# DIVORCE PARTY

*8 Ultimate Keys to Thriving*
(After All The Guests Leave)

DAVID A. YOUHAS

Copyright © 2018 David Youhas

All rights reserved- No part of this publication may be reproduced, distributed, or transmitted in any form or by any means, including photocopying, recording, or other electronic or mechanical methods, without the prior Written permission of the publisher, except in the case of brief quotations embodied in critical reviews and certain other noncommercial uses permitted by copyright law. For permission requests, write to the publisher, addressed "Attention: Permissions Coordinator,"

Get free video training, webinars, workshops, one on one coaching and complimentary offers on mastering the Divorce Party – (8 ultimate keys to thriving after all the guests leave) by registering for our email list and following our blog at:
Divorce Party - 8 Ultimate Keys to Thriving (After All the Guests Leave)
https://www.divorcepartykeys.com

ISBN: 978-1-7344174-7-0  eBook
ISBN: 978-1-7344174-0-1  Paperback

Any references to historical events, real people, or real places are used fictitiously. Names, characters, and places are products of the author's imagination.
Front cover image by Artist. Book design by David Youhas
Awaken the Mind Publishing
P.O. Box 1793
Danville, IL. 61834

*In dedication and in memory of my mother Janice Youhas ... you sacrificed almost everything to raise 5 kids as a single mother. You put us through private school while you worked and put yourself through college to become an L.P.N., then an R.N. A powerful and strong woman in spirit. Never complaining of what the world gave you and instead became empowered and choose what you would do and create in the world. You taught me that if you find your passion and serve others, your life is filled with loving relationships and unlimited potential.*

# Table of Contents

Foreword ............................................................................................ *i*
Preface .............................................................................................. *iii*
    A Brief Introduction
Chapter 1 ........................................................................................... 1
    Putting The Puzzle Pieces Of Life Back Together
Chapter 2 ........................................................................................... 9
    Quick Start Here
    The Wheel Of Life
    Plot Your Wheel Of Life Points On The W.O.L. Chart Below
Chapter 3 ......................................................................................... 19
    Spirituality
Chapter 4 ......................................................................................... 51
    Health
Chapter 5 ......................................................................................... 87
    Relationships
Chapter 6 ....................................................................................... 129
    Finances 1-2-3
Chapter 7 ....................................................................................... 163
    Personal Growth
Chapter 8 ....................................................................................... 211
    Environment
Chapter 9 ....................................................................................... 237
    Career
Chapter 10 ..................................................................................... 267
    Fun And Recreation
Conclusion ..................................................................................... 287
Afterward ....................................................................................... 291
Appendix A .................................................................................... 295
    Quotes And Scripture
Appendix B .................................................................................... 307
    Self-Development Tools
Appendix C .................................................................................... 325
Acknowledgement ......................................................................... 327
Bibliography .................................................................................. 331
About The Author ......................................................................... 333

# Foreword

David and I met years ago when he decided to become an Ontological Coach. I was one of the teachers and he was a student. I remember him from the day he walked into the room, he was tall, rather shy and asked a lot of questions. He was in his head and wanted the information and details. I can relate I am/was much like him years ago. Over the next 9 moths I got to know David really well and he quickly became one of my favorite students. He was always accountable and he loved calendars, big calendars to keep track of his life, which still makes me giggle to this day. I learned he had lost a ton of weight, been divorced, wanted more and was a sponge for knowledge. At the end of this the coaching program, we gave the students a project to do a skit or skits on our 9 months together. History was in the making to be honest and quite frankly I peed my pants at the skit. David was me, yes me, tattoos, shawl, cigarette, haircut and phone in his boobs me. He had paid such great attention that he had my mannerisms, speech, my sailor language and my tell it like it is, sarcasm down to a tee. I can still see the image in my head and it always makes me belly laugh.

Fast-forward to 2020 and David and I have worked together, coached each other and I've had the immense pleasure of watching him expand his world in leaps and bounds. David never does anything half-assed as noted above if he's in he's in full bore. He is one of the most multi-talented humans I've ever met and a fabulous source of information, empathy, compassion and accountability.

I wish I had this book when I was divorcing, and I wish my divorce had been much more like David and his former spouses. David has taken his wealth of knowledge, skills, tools, and wrapped them up nicely for anyone going through a divorce or break-up to understand and process through. He's covered a lot of areas that I personally never even thought about when I was divorcing everything from Spirituality to Fun and many things in-between. Read from the beginning or choose a chapter to start where you are currently struggling, do the exercises he's laid out and explained and I promise you'll get a lot of value and bang for your buck.

If you aren't divorcing or breaking up, great, if you are this is what you need for after all the guests leave.

David, it's been my total pleasure and honor to be your teacher, mentor, friend and clearly now student.

Oceans of Love

*Joyce Glick*

# Preface
## A Brief Introduction

"Achieve your goals, not for what they will give you, but for who you must become in order to achieve them." – Jim Rohn

I decided to write this book years after my divorce to share my experiences, successes, and failures. Most important this book is all of that learning put into a powerful structure and map that will support you cleaning up the mess of your life and move you forward to an abundant and successful future.

I have experienced a unique outcome that is different than how most divorces happen, at least, so I am told. It is not perfect, but unique and special in that, my ex-wife and I both worked well together to put our children and their care first. Although our 4 children our now adults, still, the parenting still continues. We found and continue to find, common ground to work together, to love and raise our children.

I say that it is unique, and special, and this is what others around us have said. "Wow that is awesome", "That is so wonderful that you two work together for your kids." We use language like "Hey, can we talk and get on the same page about the kids?"

Kids are experts with resourcefulness, often more so than adults, and using a technique called triangulation. This is where the person not in the conversation is misrepresented or misquoted. Adults can do this as well. After all, where do you think the kids learn this from?

The purpose for me writing this book was to share what I learned along the way. As you will see in the pages of this book I sunk myself into learning.

The bottom line, although you may not see it, hear it, or feel like it now, you have control of your life and have influence on those in your life. Negative or positive, you set things in motion in ways you may not be aware of and ESPECIALLY, not even the words you say will have as much impact as the way you think, and feel, and the actions you take.

I live in Illinois and when I first began my journey into coaching, NLP and hypnosis, I was skeptical. What I was learning seemed way, way, way, far out there and pretty "woo woo" from the cornfields and flat lands where I come from. I remember saying to myself, "this way of thinking is like the thinking they do in California and that LSD crap." That is what I use to think. So, the paragraph above may evoke in you, what it did in me. Possibly a feeling of doubt.

A statement like "the way you think and feel," has a bigger impact in your life than what you say. Seems absurd, I know. I totally get that belief, that use to be me. There is scientific evidence to support this to be true. Our thoughts are things and our thoughts manifest real and material things.

There are a couple ways to explain this and how it works is simple to illustrate and understand. The awareness and practice of this, "thoughts are things" is thousands of years old. This practice or technology has been working for a long time.

Through meditation, you can focus on your breathing and its frequency. You can "think" about your breathing. Breathe in deeply and exhale out twice as slowly. Imagine with every breath that you are breathing slower and slower. Breathing in oxygen, and that oxygen gets absorbed from your lungs into your blood stream. That oxygen gets transported through your blood, through your heart, and mind. Nourishing your heart. It's like you are breathing through your heart. Nourishing your body, strengthening it and healing it. Relax.

Real world science. Now if you were hooked up to monitors, what if I told you that your heart rate would have decreased and your blood pressure will have gone down, adding time to your life expectancy? What if I told you that imagining breathing through your heart would have a real physical body effect, that your heart rate would eventually be in sync with the rhythm of your breathing? Your thoughts caused something physical to manifest and added time to your life! This is scientifically documented and fact. All this because decreasing your blood pressure and heart rate is healthier. We will dig deeper into the nerdy-ness of those systems in your body and how they work later in the chapter about Health, and discuss how chemicals are released and suppressed in your body, and how they are activated, simply by thinking.

The second important awareness, on the importance of "thoughts are things", and how powerfully those thoughts influence or communicate non-verbally to yourself and everything around you, comes from my training in neuro-linguistic programming or N.L.P.

We will dive deep into the nerdy-ness of all that later in the chapter on Relationships, but quickly I want to illustrate the importance of something you probably are not aware of. Only 7% of communication is accomplished with words. The remaining 93% is accomplished with non-verbal communication. How you feel and the thoughts you have will trump your language as you communicate by 93%. This is why text messages and emails get us in trouble. It's simply not the most effective way to communicate.

Here is what I absolutely know about communication and relationships. There will come a time (many times) where you will be humbled (before or after) and absolutely want to have the ability to speak "into the listening of someone" You will pray to God or whoever you pray to, that your caring message and your loving intention is heard.

This could be a child headed down a path you know with certainty is not good for them. This could be with an ex-spouse about something important with the kids and that you come in peace. Or this could even be a conversation with yourself, "hey you need to pull that ass hat off your head, now!"

In those critical moments where there is an important fork in the road, or maybe the end of the road with that choice, the key to being heard, the key to harnessing the ability to speak into someone's listening, is rapport. THERE IS NO OTHER WAY.

**Rapport**

Rapport is the foundation of communication. Resistance is only lack of rapport. How you feel will never change this fact. RAPPORT, RAPPORT, RAPPORT. Always start with rapport and always go back to rapport when you are not in rapport. You are smoking crack and hallucinating, if you think your words will bail you out of lack of rapport. It will never happen. It is the intention behind the words that you come in peace and that your intentions are that you care for this person that shows up in your language and inflection and body language that communicate your intention.

You are talking to someone who isn't even there without rapport. We will get all nerdy on that later in the chapter on Relationships. Rapport is a skill that you can learn and it will change your life and relationships dramatically. Out of all my training sessions, I believe the single most valuable thing that I have learned is understanding rapport and how it opens doors, where before there was darkness and no doors existed; as well as, there is a time to be out of rapport with toxicity and things you do not value.

Now the chapter on SPIRITUALITY. This was absolutely the hardest chapter for me to write. My intention was to put the key areas in a sequence of importance, if possible. The key areas that were of most importance were to go before chapters that were possibly not as important.

For example, I thought initially that the chapter on Health should obviously come first and before everything else. Because without your health, nothing else matters. I later decided to move the chapter on Spirituality from Chapter 10 to the first chapter of the key areas, Chapter 3. I truly believe Spirituality is that important for everyone to have working well in their life, and that it is worth understanding why it is so valuable. Not in a nerdy Jesus speech but that spirituality is about LOVE (my belief). We are not worth anything to anyone else if we do not value ourselves first. Nor can we reflect that love outward if we do not see it in ourselves. You can't love anyone else if you do not love yourself. Love being a verb or action. It is like the oxygen mask on an airplane, you must first put that mask on yourself, and first nourish yourself with a breath of oxygen before you can apply it to anyone else.

I discovered just how valuable spirituality and love is, as I worked through my challenges with this chapter on how Spirituality applies to everyone. I discovered with certainty that Spirituality is even more important than Health and I can prove it! If you are not loving and caring for yourself your health will suffer as well. More on that a bit later in that chapter.

My pray that you and your family find healing, forgiveness, peace, love, and a deeper connection. You will get through this and in the future you will look back on this sliver of time that seemed painful and realize you have grown into something better for yourself and for those you love. Your happiness We must take action and have a positive intention to find these things.

Welcome to Divorce Party! This is definitely not a party about fun and enjoyment, but instead, like the wreck left over after a college frat party gone horribly wrong. As you awaken, you realize, all the guests have left, things are broken, and in disarray, something's burning, things are flipped over, things are missing and the drywall punched in. Then, the sinking feeling and realization, that you contributed to this nightmare, confusion, hopelessness, denial, and anger sets in. Where do you even start?

The purpose of the book is about healing and moving forward, after a divorce in the 8 key areas of your life. This book is a culmination of all my training, originating in performance coaching and relationship coaching.

There are 1 or 2 key purposes of this book, depending upon if you have children or not. The first purpose, if you have children, is that they deserve to be placed as a first priority in your life and in all that you do. They deserve the very best you possible. They hurt the most in a divorce. The greatest suffering for me personally, was to watch my 4 children experiencing the divorce. No matter how much I hurt, that always hurt more and deeply without understanding. The children hurt more, it's not their fault and they deserve the very best you possible. Always put your children first and always take a stand for them if anything gets in the way of that.

The last purpose of this book is to triage, where you are hurting the most and provide resources to heal fast. The book is designed to assess where you are now and where you want to be instead. Then provide you with tools, resources, and exercises to create action steps that will move you forward.

Who am I to talk on this subject and what is unique about this book? The book utilizes my cumulative experience throughout my divorce and my training in performance and relationship coaching, N.L.P., and hypnosis, to triage where it hurts the most, and how to heal and move forward from exactly wherever you are. You can read the book like a healing diagnostic book, jumping to the chapters that apply. Or the book can be read sequentially, to see the bigger picture of the value of balancing and grounding our lives as a whole. We all deserve to be happy. And our children deserve the best possible "us" that we can give them, as they are the ones that are often hurt the most, as they are torn between parents that have differences and it is all out of their control. Our children deserve to be happy and loved unconditionally.

Lastly, I want to say, as cliché as it sounds, things absolutely will get better. It is absolutely inevitable with time passing. Time heals all wounds but time does not cure having more patience. There is a saying "what we resist persists." Do you want to continue holding on to feeling hurt from the past or do you want to instead hold onto and move toward, the brighter future ahead?

Did you know that feelings only last like 90 seconds and then they are gone forever if we let them go? For a hurt feeling to last we have to choose to continue to replay that movie of that thing that was said or done to us over and over and over. And like a muscle it grows in our minds and creates neurological connections in our brain like a bad virus. Giving life to that feeling that was only 90 seconds of suffering and now turning it into a favorite hits radio channel. Anytime we want to say to ourselves we are right about that thing that happened to us, we dial into that station and broadcast the suffering over and over and over. Like picking at scabs we release that feeling again and ensure that healing takes longer. A self-inflicted hypnotic trance and living in hell.

"Tis better to have loved and lost than never to have loved at all"

- Alfred Lord Tennyson

If you have lived you have been hurt and disappointed by someone. We can't escape this fact. We can't live alone or without others help in this world. With relationships I can only know what true love is when I look at my children. In any relationship promises and commitments are made, then kept or broken building or breaking trust. If you have a relationship with anyone on the planet broken trust will happen. Including commitments with yourself. Trust can be rebuilt and if the relationship matters you will.

What we focus on expands, so it is in our best interest to focus on not where we are presently, but on what we want instead. Moving forward, what do you want instead of what you have now? What does it look like? See it now through your own eyes. What do you hear? How do you want it to feel? Now, feel it now. Drop into your future self and experience that feeling. Life is good, you are loved, and you forgive and love yourself. Let that warmth of love spread throughout your entire body, from your heart, to your shoulders and legs, to your fingertips and toes and your head. Let it radiate outward, shining light and warmth on all those that surround you.

**"And now these three remain: faith, hope and love. But the greatest of these is love."**

*- Corinthians 13:13*

Faith, Hope, Love. Find it within yourself and share it with everyone in your life.

Notes:

# DIVORCE PARTY

# CHAPTER 1
## PUTTING THE PUZZLE PIECES OF LIFE BACK TOGETHER

"Things which matter most must never be at the mercy of things which matter least."

Johann Wolfgang von Goethe

# Divorce Party as easy as 1-2-3!

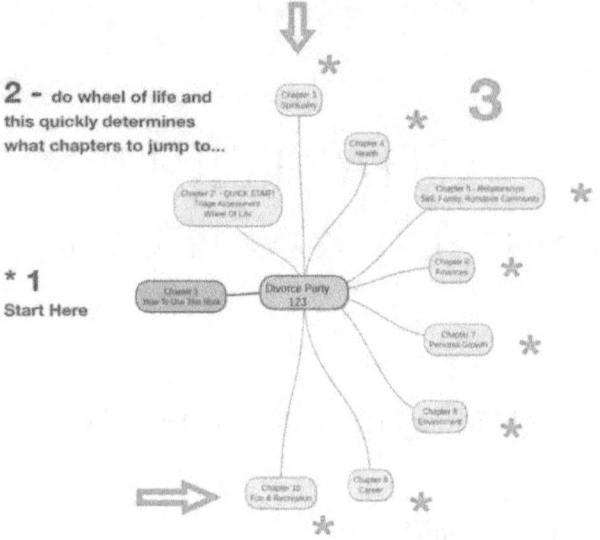

The purpose of this book... is for you to get your shit together. And more importantly, if you have children, becoming the best version of yourself possible, so you can care for your children as best as possible. If you do not have children, the purpose of this book is to help you care for yourself, and put your life back together and prosper in all the areas of your life.

Everyone on the planet has the exact same 24 hours in every day. It is what we choose as most important, and what are the most important things we want in our life that determines the quality of our life. "What we focus on expands." That being true, why not choose excellent things to focus on?

**Introduction.** Get ready to push the EASY button. I want to get you started quickly, and have you jump right into the book... right after a brief introduction. And, I want to absolutely reassure you that this book is designed to powerfully bring to the surface and identify the most challenging areas in your life out of the 8 key areas in everyone's lives.

The solution to the biggest challenges you face going through a divorce might possibly be just out of reach of your consciousness. But, as you will see, they are easy to surface, because you have clues all around you screaming their importance. This book will quickly bring to the surface where the biggest advantage is to start. It will help set you on an action path to improving those areas, to bring you to a safe place of peace and comfort, and a place of deep breathing space and freedom.

Once you know the challenging area or areas, you can skip ahead to those chapters and take action right away, quickly and effectively. In fact, right now, if you want to jump to chapter 2, you can begin the simple and quick assessing tool. And from there jump ahead to the chapters on the areas you discover you want to work on. But if you have time, I have a fascinating story to tell you.

Maybe you have found yourself here to find answers. Maybe you need to gain understanding, maybe to find something better and move in a direction toward a better life. Put simply, divorce sucks. Different people handle it different ways, but I think it fair to say, it's no party.

I have never been to a celebratory divorce party. Apparently they have them, but I know that those who pretend they are not hurting, it is only to protect their ego. And the downside of that is that we are not acknowledging the truth that we hurt. Our ego is false, we invented our ego, it's not real, and the ego only prolongs the truth. The hurt is real; the feeling of hurt needs healing inside of us.

Many people will marry their opposites. What we lack, we find attractive in another. And when we divorce, we may find ourselves needing to get proficient with skills and capabilities that we are not good at. I found myself challenged with my finances and bill paying. I literally had the money in my account, but only knew my cell phone bill was due when they would shut it off. Then the late fees and reconnect fees, and on and on. Paying my bills late only compounded my problems, stress, and more money thrown away.

I remember sitting in my house, on a hot summer evening and the power had been shut off. I'm reflecting, I can't continue to live this way. My life felt like it was out of control, even though I couldn't see it then, that I was the solution to the problem. I didn't see it that way in the middle of all of that fog of being overwhelmed, the denial, depression, confusion, embarrassment, and stubbornness.

I had been listening to this David Ramsey guy on the radio. It was fascinating how messed up people's lives were that would call in and I realized, I began to sound more and more like those callers. They were bleeding out financially and didn't have a clue. It was interesting that David had a methodology and strategy to treating the financial problem. After listening to many shows, you pretty much knew what he was going to say, usually, "sell the car if you can't afford it." Sell the $60,000 car and buy the $5000 beater that gets the job done without drowning you in debt.

I was clueless or in denial about my finances, and things were quickly getting worse and I needed help. I found a David Ramsey,

Financial Peace University class, locally and signed up. I believe the materials were around $100 and I wasn't sure I could afford even that. However, after listening to his program on the radio, I trusted him and that his promise to transform my life financially would happen.

It was one of the best decisions I made at the time. The very first class, I left with a sense and feeling of hope that things will improve financially for me, and they did absolutely. If this is your biggest challenge, get in a class now. Get online now, and sign up right now.

One of the first things I learned in the FPU class, was taking care of the 4 financial walls. And when you take care of the 4 walls, you can sleep at night.

Everyone on the planet has these 8 key areas in their life. If you are going through a divorce, some areas are going to create problems and it is well worth investing your time into resolving these problems quickly. In Chapter 2 you will do a quick and simple evaluation of your 8 key areas. It's a very simple test, in fact almost too simple to believe, but there is something about the test that really clarifies the areas you are most challenged with. Everyone's experience is different and results will vary from person-to-person.

Then you will go to the specific chapter that addresses that key area, look at resources available and what action steps to take. If you have kids, you owe it to them to do this. They hurt the most. It is your obligation and they deserve the best you, that you can be. This book will give you hope, relief, and healing so that you can focus on the most important things. The most important things precede the least important things.

I am writing this book from the perspective of a man, but my intention is that this book is a valuable resource for women and men experiencing the challenges of going through a divorce.

One last thing before we begin, forgive your trespasses. Forgiveness is usually misunderstood. I did a lot of research on forgiveness and ultimately, if you hold onto anger and hurt, you only compromise the quality of your life. I am not saying don't feel hurt, don't feel angry. I am saying that all of your feelings are absolutely valid and it's worth your health, physically and mentally, to let it go, when you are ready.

Forgiveness is not for the other person; forgiveness is for you. You are releasing that person's control over you when you forgive. You are empowering yourself when you forgive. The other person need not be present or even aware that you forgive them. Forgiveness is for you. Your health is worth it. Take a leap of faith and plant the seed of this truth in your mind. Let it grow and heal your soul.

# DIVORCE PARTY

Notes:

# Chapter 2
## Quick Start Here
## The Wheel of Life

"Too much of one thing can end up creating stress; this is something that no one needs in their life. But living a life in balance can provide harmony and peace." - Catherine Pulsifer, Birthday Wishes for a Best Friend

The origin of the wheel of life trace back to Paul J. Meyer's who founded the Success Motivation® Institute in 1960. (Meyer, 2019) Paul was seen as an industry pioneer in coaching and was a thought leader He created training programs in leadership, time management, and programs to help people achieve their goals.

**"What you vividly imagine, ardently desire, sincerely believe and enthusiastically act upon must inevitably come to pass. "**

— Paul J. Meyer

Let's get started! Life is all about balance. If we are feeling stressed, it is quite possible that we have neglected certain areas of our lives. Or maybe we relied on someone else to manage an area of our life we are not skilled in. If we put all our efforts into one area, then other areas will suffer. What if our health suffers? Does anything else matter after that?

We may have areas in our life that we are not yet skilled at. After my divorce I was challenged with organization and finances. I knew my cell phone bill was due when they shut my phone off even when I had money in my account. I then set out and found resources to build up my skills, to learn how to manage finances myself.

The wheel of life is a powerful tool. Sometimes we are so close to the problem we can only see the trees but not the forest. The wheel of life allows you to zoom out and see the big picture as an observer of your life as opposed to a player in the game.

As simple as it is, it illustrates where you are doing well and what areas are challenging. You may or may not already be aware of this. Knowledge of where your challenges are will allow you to leap to that chapter and find resources to help and move toward improving that area of your life.

Having a balanced life is like the skilled street performer. There is maintenance required to keep any one plate or all the plates spinning. If you focus too much on certain plates and not others, plates are going to slow down, wobble, then crash. The wheel of life tool helps to see and feel what areas are wobbling or have crashed.

When clients come to me for coaching, NLP or hypnosis work, it is usually that one or more of these key areas of their life is wobbling or plates have crashed. And even more importantly, without the plate of health, none of the other plates even matter.

A balanced life supports and nourishes the other areas of your life. What may seem like something you do not have enough time for, may become the realization that time doesn't even matter if you do not care for yourself first. Nothing else matters.

Here is the good news. It is easier to take baby steps that build momentum. How does someone achieve that balance, have enough time and money to keep all the plates spinning? When you value mindfulness and care of the plates, you see that it is much easier to keep the plates maintained and spinning.

The momentum of a rhythm and maintenance, or with purposefulness and intention, is less effort and less expenditure of time and money. In other words, you can't afford the loss of time and money it takes to dig plates out of wobbling ruts. It is so much easier to intentionally maintain the plates.

You will find and be surprised how much more money and time you have when you are not paying the non-maintenance tax. The NSF fees associated with lack of maintenance are a wake -up call to take action.

Now we will begin to assess 8 different key areas. Rate the key area from -10 to +10, from least satisfied to most satisfied. Trust your unconscious mind, select and complete all 8 key areas now.

Health

0 1 2 3 4 5 6 7 8 9 10

Relationships

0 1 2 3 4 5 6 7 8 9 10

Finances

0 1 2 3 4 5 6 7 8 9 10

Personal Growth

0 1 2 3 4 5 6 7 8 9 10

Environment

0 1 2 3 4 5 6 7 8 9 10

Career

0 1 2 3 4 5 6 7 8 9 10

Recreation

0 1 2 3 4 5 6 7 8 9 10

Spirituality

0 1 2 3 4 5 6 7 8 9 10

Notes:

_____

_____

_____

_____

_____

# Plot your wheel of life points on the W.O.L. chart below

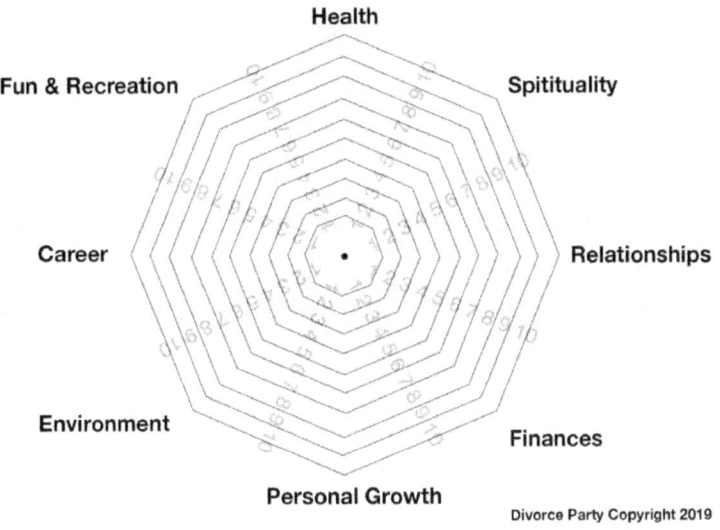

Now prioritize the list from least satisfied to most satisfied below. Enter the least satisfied key area on the number 1. Line below and continue the list from least satisfied to most satisfied.

1. _____
2. _____
3. _____
4. _____
5. _____
6. _____

7. _____

8. _____

9. _____

10. _____

Now that you can clearly see the areas with the most growth opportunity, jump ahead to those chapters and get started! All of the different chapters will offer insights, tips, help, and healing. At the beginning of each of the key area chapters, there will be an overview of the value of that key area. For example, do any other key areas even matter if our health is failing? I intentionally put the health chapter first because nothing else matters if you don't have your health.

And one last disclaimer, if you find something abrasive, it is not my intention to be harmful, and I encourage you to take a very close look at that. If something pushes a button in you, try to step outside of yourself and be an observer of yourself and ask how did that cause a reaction in you. Truth can hurt and it's worth it, otherwise we are living in a delusion.

An example of this, that is abrasive to me as well, is when I play the victim card and someone calls me on my own stuff. "Get over yourself." Ouch, that hurts. I'm not saying that bad stuff doesn't happen to good people, I'm saying, so what, now what are you going to do about it instead?

Playing the victim card. Choosing to be the victim, staying a victim, wallowing around in wanting to be right that you are a victim, rolling around in your own feces proclaiming "look what has been done to me," moaning and groaning and bitching "look at me, I am a victim!" This is not an empowering state and it is a choice that you make. To remove ourselves from this situation or "victim" state, we have to choose something different. We can make a different choice. We can choose to be an advocate of our own choices and that will empower us. You see, WE DO NOT HAVE CONTROL OVER ANYONE BUT OURSELVES. When you get that, your life will change.

We are either in a state of cause or effect and it's a choice you get to make. We are either the cause of our destiny or at the effect of others, and you are the only person on the planet that has that power over yourself.

**"Too much sanity may be madness and maddest of all: to see life as it is, and not as it should be!"** - the Man of La Mancha

Notes:

_____

_____

_____

_____

_____

_____

_____

_____

_____

_____

# CHAPTER 3
## SPIRITUALITY

**For believers, nonbelievers and the not sure**

"God speaks loudly in the moments between silence"

"I don't mind so much, a minister condemning my soul to eternal hell, as long as he has tears of sadness in his eyes, but not tears of joy"

Jim Rohn

"The atoms of our bodies are traceable to stars that manufactured them in their cores and exploded these enriched ingredients across our galaxy, billions of years ago. For this reason, we are biologically connected to every other living thing in the world. We are chemically connected to all molecules on Earth. And we are atomically connected to all atoms in the universe. We are not figuratively, but literally stardust." - Neil deGrasse Tyson

**What I hope for you in this chapter**

✓ Spirituality is about Love

✓ Spirituality is more important than health,

I can prove it

✓ Forgiveness starts with forgiving yourself

✓ Why to forgive others and what's in it for you

✓ 7 Deadly Sins

✓ Quit beating yourself up - shame and guilt

✓ Love yourself first, otherwise, we can't

love others

✓ Get connected – we are more than ourselves

✓ You are loved, you deserve that love,

✓ be courageous enough to accept it

✓ Good and Evil and Revenge

✓ Live and let live

✓ This storm will pass. The sun returns,

spring follows winter, every time!

✓ Mindful Breathing

This chapter is, in my belief, the most important chapter of all for you, for me, for everyone. Not in a cheesy, evangelical selling you God way. I am not going to ask you to hold hands and sing Kumbaya. I truly believe that spirituality not only applies to you and to everyone else, but that it is the most important element in your life, whether you know it or not.

Spirituality is about love and if you do not love yourself the rest of your life and everyone in it will not matter, inside and out. Spirituality is about love. How would a world look, feel, and sound without love? As messed up as the world can seem to be, without love, I can't even imagine what a different experience it would be.

I am not a licensed therapist and I do believe in them. If you are experiencing any medically diagnosed symptoms, or anything that feels like too much, please reach out and get help. There is no shame in admitting when we need help. If you need help, get it.

I was raised Catholic and presently consider myself a Christian. Whatever you believe or do not believe, wherever you are at, or not at in your spiritual journey, please stay for a while, and stay as long as you like. Everyone is welcome here. This is a safe, peaceful, caring, healing, and loving space. I hope this chapter reaches out to you, touches you somehow and that you know and feel you are loved and that we are connected. I hope that you feel you exist, you have experienced love, you are loved, you are deserving of love and there is opportunity to share that love with others.

**Disclaimers Before We Proceed**

I have some disclaimers for everyone in this chapter. For the atheists, agnostics, and the Christians.

#1. I consider myself a Christian. I am but a student in Christianity, and by no means an expert or pretend to be an expert.

#2. The examples or quoted scriptures I use are not intended to get you to drink the Kool aid or to convert you. It is just that the stories are so relevant and powerful and directly apply to today's life. Why not learn the curiously similar lessons of life, at someone else's expense who has already been there and done that?

In fact as humans we are perpetually reliving these Jungian archetypes. We are continually recycling the hero's journey and all its intricacies, roles, feelings, attitudes, identities, capabilities, behaviors, and outcomes. Why not look at the cheat sheet for life and cliff notes from human success and failure. Real experiences through metaphors. They have enough value to have survived and still exist at our fingertips because someone wrote them down! Hopefully and intentionally we learn in advance, where we still have choices and we still have time to make the best educated guess.

There are fascinating, incredible examples, wisdom, stories and metaphors. They are just so excellent to illuminate the human condition and dramas of life. The good, the bad, and the ugly. And often these metaphors are an illumination to see a way out, or how to avoid or escape the snare. It is fascinating how well the stories apply to everyone's lives and modern-day life. Like a time-machine, you get to see how the story, does or does not work out in advance. We are blind by our own ignorance, often and the wisdom in the metaphors are valuable information.

### Spirituality is Love

Everyone has different beliefs concerning spirituality. My belief is Christian. And if we are talking Christian spirituality, the challenge or the argument is "show me evidence, show me proof that God exists." There is a reason it's called 'faith' and my belief comes from my experiences and a feeling. This chapter is not about trying to convince you that God exists, but instead, that spirituality is something I believe we all can have in common, a need for love.

Spirituality for the atheist or agnostic or other beliefs, does exist. I have witnessed it within and outside of them. Selfless acts, caring empathy, giving and sharing, accepting and giving love. I have seen incredible heart-felt love, genuine gratitude, authentic compassion, tears and heart-felt human empathy and a longing to be connected and to connect.

I believe spirituality is about Love. And love is a human need. A baby that is not held, touched, or hugged at birth will stop growth and if continued to be denied touch, denied love, that baby will die. You do not need to believe in God to have empathy for that aloneness.

**Spirituality is more important than health, I can prove it.**

The darkest moment of my life, I was about to end my life. That's where I found myself, lying in bed and with the means to accomplish it. I was so deeply sad and crying and alone. Power shut off, house being foreclosed on, jobless and was about to become homeless. I had painted myself into a corner. I finally realized where I was at this point in my life, and now to visit my kids on my weekend, I would not have a place called home or a place for them to visit. I don't know, maybe a park? I was so sad at that realization; how did I not care enough about them to allow this to happen? How did I let myself get into this horrible place? How did I not see this inevitable coming?

I prayed for a reason to live. I am pretty sure, this is what they call 'rock bottom', definitely the lowest point I had ever felt in my life. A feeling without worth. There was this continual sadness that was like a constant tone, a gnawing tooth ache, of the loss of what I felt was home. Not just the structure but what happened there. The relationship and meaning of what a home is. Again, I prayed for a reason to live. Believer in God or not, we all have free will. That is the only thing we control in this world. Our choices. We do not control the choices of others but we absolutely control our own choices, 100%, every time. Yesterday, today, and tomorrow. We are driving the bus.

I had a shift from grieving and sadness to the realization of how I contributed to put myself exactly where I was at. I put myself into this situation clearly by my own choices.

Something unusual began to happen. I was paying attention to the moment and how I was feeling. I could hear my breath. It seemed loud in the silence, slow and deep. Living out in the country it was all I could hear. I felt a soothing warmth and calmness spreading throughout my entire body that was contrasting the moment of what I had been feeling and the reason I was in my bed. The things that seemed devastating, didn't matter anymore. It was laughable how important I had made them and how unimportant they were.

There is a coaching presupposition that says "what we resist, persists." I had been convinced I was the victim of my circumstances, as if the world was happening to me and I had no choices. However, it is not what happens to us, it is what we do in response that makes the difference. We do not control the world happening; spring, summer, fall, or winter. But we do have influence on our outcomes. By learning awareness, we become attune to life happening and the choices to be prepared for winter and that spring returns again. Every time.

I had made choices in the past that got me exactly where I was at this moment, lying in my bed. And I began to look forward and past this moment. What would I need to do to turn it around? I work with clients where I will ask, where do you want to be in 1 year, 3 years, 5 years, 10 years and a 'deer in the headlights' look will often appear. However, in this moment, I felt completely aware of what I needed to do, the steps I needed to take, to turn this all around. I saw a way out from the moment I was in, and a future restored. Life had felt so heavy. Like trying to swim while holding bags of concrete. And it was as easy as letting the things that were pulling me down go. Deciding to open my hands and not hold onto being right, or righteous...

"No temptation has overtaken you except what is common to mankind. And God is faithful; he will not let you be tempted beyond what you can bear. But when you are tempted, he will also provide a way out so that you can endure it."

**Corinthians 10-13**

*The lifesaving value for me - There is always a way out of the snare, provided you are looking for it and take action on it.*

I knew that I was exhausted physically. I knew that I needed to improve my physical and mental health. I took deep, slow breaths and enjoyed the feeling of life, focus, and the nourishment they gave me. I went on to restore my health and loose over 100 pounds, and run 6 marathons in 2 years. I got an apartment so that I could see my kids and have a place to call home. And then purchased a house and paid the mortgage off in 6-years time. Were my prayers answered? I believe they were.

### Forgiveness starts with forgiving yourself

I have heard it said before that what we see wrong in others is something we see wrong in ourselves. What we do not like in others is something we don't like in ourselves. When I first heard this, I resisted that this was even a possibility. It even bothered and angered me even. I thought this is a trick, the offender was using on me.

And then I heard this... I had heard it a hundred times before but I never "heard" and felt the meaning before.

**"Why do you look at the speck of sawdust in your brother's eye and pay no attention to the plank in your own eye? How can you say to your brother, 'Let me take the speck out of your eye,' when all the time there is a plank in your own eye? You hypocrite, first take the plank out of your own eye, and then you will see clearly to remove the speck from your brother's eye."**

Mathew 7:3-5

Again, not selling you the God Kool Aid here. I am, however, continually amazed how this body of work, the Bible, speaks to me. How it speaks to me over time. I had heard that message and could even recite it. Obviously, it was important enough for me to get because I had heard it so many freaking times. It was as if, those who loved me knew I wouldn't get it at first or the first several hundred times. But when I was ready for the message, to hear it, and feel it, it was there all along to save me from the snare.

I will go as far as to say it's almost spooky. My belief in God has come and gone and returned, weakened and strengthened over time. Perhaps you have had moments of serendipity, or moments where all of the universe came together at one focal point in your life that shook you so profoundly in a way that left you in awe, as this can't be a coincidence. Whatever it is, I want to encourage you, to invite that caring love into your life and to integrate it with everything in your life.

My belief now is that we project ourselves outward into the world. When I see something I do not like, I see it as an opportunity to reflect on, how is this happening in my life? How can I become a better person, or how can I love myself? How can I forgive myself and how can I forgive others? The flip side of this is that when you see something good in the world it is that it is something you see in yourself.

Forgiveness starts with forgiving yourself. We can be our worst enemy and our worst critic. We may not even realize we are being so critical of ourselves. If we look out into the world and are frustrated with how others are behaving, the bigger question is, how do you see yourself behaving this way? How are you negatively self-talking about that behavior you see in yourself?

I know this fictional guy I made up for this example, who is a perfectionist and it can be so horribly annoying. He demands perfection out of everyone else and if you fall short, he is over-the-top critical and gets over-the-top angry. The best part is, he is far from the perfect he demands from everyone else, he attempts to hide his own imperfections, or denies them, and it is obvious to everyone but himself. Perfectionism is a fraud, as we can never become perfect. We can strive towards excellence but we can never obtain being perfect. There is always room for healthy improvement.

You have seen this guy or girl, right? How do you deal with them so they don't create such turbulence in your life? Well, if they are only a projection of what I see in myself... (ouch) then I want to ask some questions about everything I see wrong in them, that I actually see wrong in myself.

How is it that I am trying to be perfect in my life in a delusional and toxic way? How am I a fraud? How do I find myself annoying to myself and others? How do I demand perfection from myself and others? How do I frustrate others when I am demanding perfection? How do I try to hide my imperfection? How can I do my best and accept myself for doing my best? How do I know when I am doing my best? How can others who depend on me, forgive me when I am not being at my best? How can I forgive myself for being human just like everyone else on the planet? How do I appreciate myself? How do I care for myself? How do I love myself?

We are not our past and we are not our future. We are our choices. And that we do control, in the moment of right now. At any moment we can make a new choice to set in motion a new way of being. In that way we can design our future by the choices we make right now. If you are not happy with past choices and past outcomes, that is okay. Forgive yourself and keep moving forward. We can't change the past. If we have hurt others, and the relationship is important enough, then we want to rebuild trust in that relationship. (More on how to do that in the chapter on relationships.) Take the lessons learned from the past and make new choices for different future outcomes; results that are in your favor, what you value and what you desire. Forgive yourself, learn from the past and make new choices moving forward.

**Why forgive others and what's in it for you**

*"Resentment is like taking poison and waiting for the other person to die."*

Malachy McCourt

What have I learned about forgiveness to keep my sanity? I was raised Catholic and yet somehow, I missed out on what forgiveness really is and why it is so important. I must have had some warped version that was imposed upon me.

Basically, my version was that you had to forgive others and then keep on living with the person you can't stand. And once you forgave them, you could never bring it up again regardless of how you felt. I especially didn't like that last part. As it seemed contradictory to forgive because that's what God wants me to do, and yet it seems like lying to yourself about how you really feel should be just as important in God's eyes as lying to someone else.

I had a problem with forgiving. And it was affecting my health physically and emotionally. I was on a journey to remake myself and had just discovered audio books. And sure enough, there were books on forgiveness.

1. Forgiveness is not for the other person. It is not about them. It is about freeing yourself from being bound to sin... anger, hurt, hate, jealousy, etc. (see 7 deadly sins.)

2. The other person does not even need to know you are forgiving them. Again, this isn't about them. It is about you letting go of the shit in your head.

3. "I thought you forgave me?" Sometimes we have to keep on, keepin' on... forgiving. Something happens that re-triggers a hurt, we have to repeat the forgiving. It may never fully go away. It will get easier, lighter and the hurt will move farther and drift away. With time, drifting farther and farther away until it no longer has you bound.

4. Just because we forgive someone, does not entitle them to receive our trust, companionship, or the gift of our presence. Some relationships are toxic. It is okay to move on. You owe yourself to forgiveness to release your sin. You do not owe someone else your trust if they have broken it.

5. Be accountable for your own stupidity and personal choices that delivered you to get what you got. In other words, no matter how jacked up the situation is, your best thinking got you there. In every failure, let down, and lesson in life, there is ALWAYS the seed of opportunity for you to learn and God will provide you a way out. This out requires that you personally be accountable for your choices and follow his guide. You must take action and act upon the way out.

### 7 Deadly Sins

**Pride** is excessive belief in one's own abilities, that interferes with the individual's recognition of the grace of God. It has been called the sin from which all others arise. Pride is also known as Vanity.

**Envy** is the desire for others' traits, status, abilities, or situation.

**Gluttony** is an inordinate desire to consume more than that which one requires.

**Lust** is an inordinate craving for the pleasures of the body.

**Anger** is manifested in the individual who spurns love and opts instead for fury. It is also known as Wrath.

**Greed** is the desire for material wealth or gain, ignoring the realm of the spiritual. It is also called Avarice or Covetousness.

**Sloth** is the avoidance of physical or spiritual work.

## Quit beating yourself up - shame and guilt

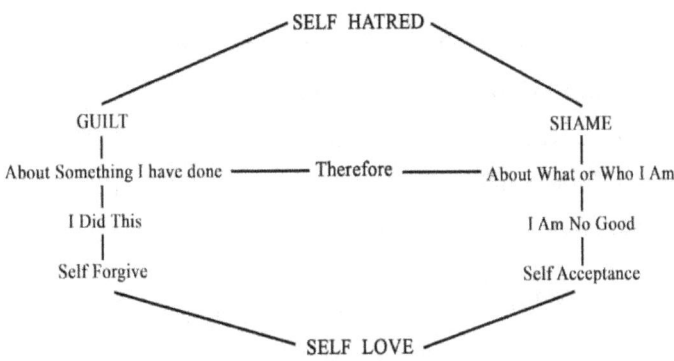

If beating yourself up over something that happened in the past had any value, I would be on board with saying keep on doing it. However, there is not any value to be stuck in a past, you can't change. There is no value gained by dwelling in the past. Just a brief observation for truth in details to learn from it. We can't change the past, and we are not our past. BUT there is a message from the experience we do want to get. There is a lesson to learn and then move on, move forward.

It seems like there are some people, who like to see others torturing themselves. "You should feel bad," spoken with seriousness and a peculiar slight smile of pleasure. They seem to enjoy watching someone inflicting pain on themselves, and they remind them continually of why they should. There are toxic narcissists, sociopaths at the very least and sad, miserable people, who enjoy seeing pain and suffering in others.

If you look around them, they surround themselves with a black hole of sadness, people who feel bad about themselves. We want to design our circle of relationships, surround ourselves with people that lift us up and leave us feeling good about ourselves. We become like the 5 people we hang around the most. Choose wisely.

What is the value of feeling bad about the past? Shame and guilt have a place and a purpose. They are usually a negative emotion where we feel bad about ourselves. They are an important part of our social intelligence. Like the white lines on the road, they keep us in our lane, they hurt when we cross over and away from our values.

There is appropriate and not appropriate guilt. If someone says you are a bad person or parent, the concern is that you don't feel shame and guilt for someone else's opinion or belief that is not yours and not even true. Or what about negative self-talk? What if you listen to your negative self-talk carefully, and you realize you are just replaying an old out-of-date tape recording, of what someone else said to you when you were a child that you believed, and wasn't and still isn't true.

What if you were driving and the person next to you in the car, let out a blood curdling scream with conviction, "You are on the wrong side of the road!" For a split second you might wonder if it is true. Or your primal instinct may even have you instantaneously react and swerve.

What if what they are saying isn't true? What others say does in fact affect us and our beliefs about ourselves on a subconscious level. Truth begins with challenging what is true. Challenge the validity of what is said and how you feel around people close to you. Is this person someone I trust? Is there any truth in what they are saying?

**The Circus Elephant**

Once upon a time, there was a circus elephant. When he was a baby, his leg was tied to a small spike in the ground. The baby elephant pulls and pulls and pulls, but could not escape. He wants to explore the world and all the exciting things going on around him. And he can only imagine the incredible things that must be happening beyond what he can see. He pulls and pulls but cannot go beyond his limitation. Eventually and slowly over time the baby elephant goes from thinking he can escape to knowing he is at his limits, knowing he has no freedom outside of the length of that chain. Nothing exists outside of his parameter. His world, his reality exists within the confines of that small, small, small space.

The elephant grows up to become a massive and strong adult, believing there is no freedom outside of that chain length and this is a lie that someone else gave him. Although he is beyond strong enough and could easily pull a tree and its roots out of the ground. This little, tiny, small spike, a belief from the past, the size of a toothpick in comparison to his body size and weight, out leverages the elephants powerful massive strength. The belief is out of date and not even true with who the elephant is in the present. And the belief is as invisible as the sky is blue and fire is hot.

How are we like the elephant? How have we gone through life holding onto an invisible belief? Are we not capable to do something, because we failed at it sometime in the past? How are we held back by the past with out of date beliefs that no longer serve us? How have we avoided trying something new because of a belief we have said or that someone else told us? How are we holding back because of someone else's limiting beliefs in what they could or could not do? Do you want to uncover and update your belief system and take action toward creating the life you want?

I have heard it said that "there is always a little bit of truth to everything said," even a negative message. But it is not all of the truth. Nor is it the end of the truth and successes yet come. You may have done something unfavorable, but it is not fully who you are or who you are becoming. We are not our past and **we choose** our future. Begin to notice the messages that people are sending you, both positive and negative, and challenge the validity without a response. Challenge the relationship with this person. Is this someone you trust and know to absolutely care for you?

If we internalize judgment from someone else, and feel bad for how someone else believes we are or how we should be, that is our own choice. If you have ever said "that person makes me feel... X" More on that in the chapter on relationships. No one else can make us feel anything without us choosing to feel it. There is a stimulation (stimulus) and our choice of a response, action, or feeling.

What blocks loving self and loving others? Many things, including shame and guilt. If not challenged or clarified as appropriate or not, this can become devastatingly toxic. Guilt and shame sometimes are experienced one with the other and sometimes the terms are used interchangeably. However, they are quite different.

**New Oxford American Dictionary** (Jewell & Abate, 2010) **defines guilt and shame as:**

*Guilt - a feeling of having done wrong or failed in an obligation. The fact of having committed a specified or implied offense or crime.*

*Shame - a painful feeling of humiliation or distress caused by the consciousness of wrong or foolish behavior.*

One feeling relies on empathy for others and the other one involves feelings about oneself. Both can be appropriate or not appropriate.

What if the guilt comes from outside of us, from judgment from another, and we believe it comes from within us? What if our environment or relationships have told us who we should be or how we should behave, even though it is against our values? What if this happened at a very young age and we have been so conditioned to believe it, we accept it as truth? It is worth questioning our beliefs because they are just below consciousness and accepted as truths.

*Look for these preloaded judgment words like -* **should, ought, must.** *They will indicate or red flag what follows to be suspect and judgmental in nature, that we or others are judging others or ourselves*

Be accountable for your choices, take ownership of your choices and question the statement given: *You should be a better parent!* Am I a bad parent? Am I a perfect parent? How can I improve my parenting? Everyone has room for improvement. Am I doing the best I can? How can I add value to my parenting? What good things am I already doing to be a good parent?

Guilt that turns to shame can become toxic because it can limit us to our own awareness of what is real about ourselves. It can limit us with what we are fully capable of doing. If we believe we are not a good person, we set ourselves up to potentially be less than we are as a human being.

We want to get clarity on the message from guilt and then move on. We make mistakes, we learn from our mistakes. We are human. But the truth is, we can't change the past. If we have done something to hurt ourselves or somebody else, then we want to be accountable for our choices and move on. We do not want to let ourselves get stuck in a past we can't change. The very best we can do is to learn from our experiences, make new choices in the future, and keep moving forward.

There is more on rebuilding trust and accountability in the chapter on relationships. We communicate commitments/promises, and keep them or break them. We either build trust or tear it down. This includes trusting others or others trusting us. Trust can absolutely be rebuilt.

**Love yourself first, otherwise, we can't love others**

Earlier in this chapter we talked about that what we see outside of ourselves, is simply a reflection of what we see within in ourselves. If you see something in someone that pushes your buttons, it is only because you see that inside yourself as something that you do not like about yourself. If you see something in someone that you admire, it is only a reflection of something you admire about yourself; something that you value in yourself.

If someone gives selflessly to another person and this warms your heart, you say now that is a good person, I like them. You are projecting your reality onto them. What you see is only a reflection of you.

The world isn't broken and neither are we. We can try to fix the world that appears broken and yet, it is only a reflection of what we see in ourselves. The fascinating truth is that the more work we do on ourselves, the more good things we see in the world. Nothing has changed in the world, but yet it appears to have changed. It's that our glasses or lenses that filter how we see the world has changed.

And when I say work on ourselves, I do not mean fixing ourselves, but accepting ourselves as human and not perfect. We make mistakes and we learn, and grow and move forward. Loving ourselves is accepting ourselves for who we are and how we have been. And as we work on loving ourselves more and more, we see the world as a different place. We cannot love others if we do not love ourselves first. We can only see in the world a reflection of what we already see inside of ourselves. Love yourself first so you can reflect that love and light into the darkness of the world and you will see that love projected all around you.

**Get connected – we are more than ourselves**

In Maslow's Hierarchy of Needs, the 3rd level of self-actualization is Love and Belonging. This includes: friendship, intimacy, family, and a sense of connection. There is more to life than just ourselves. It is built in us to be connected to others. I am an introvert and even still, I know the value to be around others. We cannot do life alone, even if we feel we want to be alone.

Feelings of shame can drive us into isolation, a place worth occasionally visiting for reflection, but not a place to live. It was the realization that I was making everything about me, and in that loneliness, I was actually pushing away and hurting everyone, those who loved me the most. Those who had the best possibility for me to see I had an incredible purpose and reason for loving life.

**You are loved, you deserve that love,**

**be courageous enough to accept it**

I had experienced depression and this is the main reason for writing this book. The paradox of depression. It's as if there is a gap between the person experiencing depression and the help they need from others; between the vast darkness and not even seeing the love and light just outside of them and all around them.

You are surrounded by people that love you and want to help you, but they probably don't know how. There is this gap that needs to be bridged and it has to be initiated by the person in the darkness. Easier said than done.

There seem to be all kinds of reasons to not ask for others help; pride, shame, fear. A bridge can be built between the you and those that love you. You are loved. Building this bridge begins with surrendering to loving yourself and allowing others to love you, and that you need and want help.

I parable from the bible that reminds me of how I felt experiencing being lost in depression and returning to those that loved me. This is the parable of the lost son. I remember sitting in church many times as tears streamed down my face as I realized just how foolish I had been to deny love in my life.

**The Parable of the Lost Son**

**11** Jesus continued: "There was a man who had two sons. **12** The younger one said to his father, 'Father, give me my share of the estate.' So, he divided his property between them. 13 "Not long after that, the younger son got together all he had, set off for a distant country and there squandered his wealth in wild living. 14 After he had spent everything, there was a severe famine in that whole country, and he began to be in need. 15 So he went and hired himself out to a citizen of that country, who sent him to his fields to feed pigs. 16 He longed to fill his stomach with the pods that the pigs were eating, but no one gave him anything. 17 "When he came to his senses, he said, 'How many of my father's hired servants have food to spare, and here I am starving to death! 18 I will set out and go back to my father and say to him: Father, I have sinned against heaven and against you. 19 I am no longer worthy to be called your son; make me like one of your hired servants.' 20 So he got up and went to his father. "But while he was still a long way off, his father saw him and was filled with compassion for him; he ran to his son, threw his arms around him and kissed him.

21 "The son said to him, 'Father, I have sinned against heaven and against you. I am no longer worthy to be called your son.' 22 "But the father said to his servants, 'Quick! Bring the best robe and put it on him. Put a ring on his finger and sandals on his feet. 23 Bring the fattened calf and kill it. Let's have a feast and celebrate. 24 For this son of mine was dead and is alive again; he was lost and is found.' So, they began to celebrate. 25 "Meanwhile, the older son was in the field. When he came near the house, he heard music and dancing. 26 So he called one of the servants and asked him what was going on. 27 'Your brother has come,' he replied, 'and your father has killed the fattened calf because he has him back safe and sound.' 28 "The older brother became angry and refused to go in. So his father went out and pleaded with him. 29 But he

answered his father, 'Look! All these years I've been slaving for you and never disobeyed your orders. Yet you never gave me even a young goat so I could celebrate with my friends. **30** But when this son of yours who has squandered your property with prostitutes comes home, you kill the fattened calf for him!'

**31** "'My son,' the father said, 'you are always with me, and everything I have is yours. **32** But we had to celebrate and be glad, because this brother of yours was dead and is alive again; he was lost and is found.'" Luke 15:11-32 NIV

### Good and Evil and Revenge

Does good and evil exist? Yes. And don't even entertain it. Moving forward in our life requires us to focus on what we control in this world, our own choices and actions. If someone has wronged us, we want to turn the other cheek and forgive them. Forgive them again and again and again, as long as it takes to get that evil out of our heart.

If you entertain evil, you are only allowing evil into your heart. Even allowing evil thoughts have a way to manifest as things, as thoughts are things. By thinking of hurting others with thoughts, words or actions, you are only hurting yourself. Let karma, the universe or God deal with them or like a boomerang that evil will return in abundance to you.

**Revenge...**

**Beloved, never avenge yourselves, but leave it to the wrath of God, for it is written, "Vengeance is mine, I will repay, says the Lord."**

- Romans 12:19 ESV / 172

### Live and let live

There is a distinction between judging things and accepting things for what they are. For example, we could judge someone for who we think they should be. Remember that the word "should" is a red flag word that means that judgment follows after it in a statement.

We fall in love and the chemicals that affect our judgment blind us for about two years. And thus, this is where the saying came from that "love is blind." Then we see the person truthfully for the first time, for who they really are. Or maybe we see ourselves truthfully for the first time and we don't like what we see. We see ourselves in a reflection of someone else, how we have hurt someone else and we realize we don't want to be that reflection.

Back to falling in love and judging others. When we finally see someone for the first time without judgment, to judge someone else, is to believe they have changed and that they are not the same person we first met. We want them to be the old person we thought they were and should be or act the way we think they should.

However, we are seeing them for who they are. It could be possibly the values they hold dear and do not conflict with our own. Mother nature had good intentions putting blinders on us so that we would survive as a species and reproduce.

The following metaphor speaks to seeing people for who they really are and not judging right or wrong, but just what is. Rocks are hard and water is wet. It just is what it is. The intention is not to try and remake anyone wrong or to say who someone that we think they should be rather than who they truly are. We have big enough timbers in our own eyes and lives to worry about. That is what we want to put our focus on; the things we control in our lives so that we can thrive and stay alive.

### The story of the frog and the scorpion

One day a scorpion and a frog happen to meet on the bank of the river at the same time. The frog was about to jump in the river and swim to the other side, but before he jumps, the scorpion comes up to negotiate. The scorpion says: "Mr. Frog, it has always been my dream to get to the other side of the river and I am a scorpion and I can't swim. Would you be so generous to let me hop on your back, and you swim across the river and transport me to the other side so that I can fulfill my destiny?" The frog gets to thinking, and says: "No way! Scorpions sting frogs and kill them. I would get halfway out there where the water is too deep, you would sting me and I would drown. That's not going to happen today or any day my friend." The scorpion shook his head and said to the frog: "You're not thinking right with your tiny frog mind you were given. Think about it logically. If I stung you out there, yes you would die, but so would I! I'm not interested in committing suicide, I just want to get to the other side to finally see what life has to offer, maybe greener pastures. Please take me, it has always been my dream since I was a little scorpion," as a tear began to form in the scorpion's eye. And the frog says: "OK, OK, OK, that makes sense. Hop on on and we will get you to the other side." So, the frog turns around and the scorpion hops on the frog's back and the frog starts off across the river. The frog is swimming and sure enough half way across the scorpion stings the frog. The toxin begins to paralyze the frog and the frog is struggling to stay above water. Going down 2nd, 3rd, now 4th time, the frog can't believe the situation. He asks the scorpion: "Why did you do that? Not just me, but we both are going to die!" And the scorpion calmly replies: "Because I am a scorpion and that's what scorpions do. Scorpions sting frogs."

**The storm will pass, the sun will return,**

**spring follows winter every time**

*"Three things will last forever: faith, hope, and love - and the greatest of these is love."*

Corinthians 13 -13

If you think it's impossible, it isn't

If you think you know everything, you don't...

If you think you're alone, you're not...

- Jim Rohn

It is easy for me to say things will absolutely get better because they have for me. And they absolutely will for you. I also remember wanting to punch every do-gooder in the face or slap them for their positive attitude. So, in that way, I apologize for stating what seems obvious to me, and maybe not yet for you. I am sorry for all your hurt. It's not yours to hold onto it is yours to set free. Let it go and give it to me or God or the water or release it to the wind. Let it drift away. Far, far, far away until it vanishes over the horizon. Breathe deep and let it out twice as slow. Let your breath heal your mind, body, spirit and your heart.

I am with you on this. I am here with you now. I have been exactly where you are and so many others have also that have made it across to the other side to celebrate that life is good and you are loved. I am beside you on your journey as you will see, hear and feel things improving as you take action steps moving forward. I am also on the other side with you in the future. We are celebrating and how does that feel now that you have come so far?

I want to encourage you to let go of how things improving is going to happen, but know that it absolutely will happen. It really just takes patience and like it or not, things will improve. There is a saying that "what we focus on expands." I have this saying strategically placed in my house for me to see, multiple times throughout the day. It's the first and last thing I see, when I wake up and before I go to bed.

Anytime my life seems to have turned upside down, I ask myself "how am I focusing on this energy that I do not want in my life and what is it that I want instead"? That is possibly the most important question you can ask yourself to get you out of where you do not want to be.

Wherever you are at in life, if you don't like how life feels, ask "how do I want to feel instead"? If you are not happy with your career, ask yourself, "how do I want my career to look like or feel like or sound like instead"? The answer to that question is the work to do, "what do you want instead"?

Obviously, you know how to ask, and look at and focus on what you don't want. Stop that! Ask "what do you want instead?" You will begin to notice more and more opportunities, experiences, and resources that will support you in what you do want. Act as if the universe wants you to be successful and it will.

**Mindful Breathing**

(Vivyan, 2009)

The primary goal of mindful breathing is simply a calm, non-judging awareness, allowing thoughts and feelings to come and go without getting caught up in them.

- Sit comfortably, with your eyes closed and your spine reasonably straight.

- Bring your attention to your breathing.

- Imagine that you have a balloon in your tummy. Every time you breathe in, the balloon inflates. Each time you breathe out, the balloon deflates. Notice the sensations in your abdomen as the balloon inflates and deflates. Your abdomen rising with the in-breath, and falling with the out-breath.

- Thoughts will come into your mind, and that's okay, because that's just what the human mind does. Simply notice those thoughts, then bring your attention back to your breathing.

- Likewise, you can notice sounds, physical feelings, and emotions, and again, just bring your attention back to your breathing.

- You don't have to follow those thoughts or feelings, don't judge yourself for having them, or analyze them in any way. It's okay for the thoughts to be there. Just notice those thoughts, and let them drift on by, bringing your attention back to your breathing.

- Whenever you notice that your attention has drifted off and is becoming caught up in thoughts or feelings, simply note that the attention has drifted, and then gently bring the attention back to your breathing. It's okay and natural for thoughts to enter into your awareness, and for your attention to follow them. No matter how many times this happens, just keep bringing your attention back to your breathing.

**Final thoughts on Spirituality**

If you do not believe in God, or a higher power, or you are undecided, I want to encourage you to continue to pursue love. Love is a verb. Love for yourself and love for others.

What is something you want to work on with your spirituality? Complete a S.M.A.R.T. Goal for what you want to improve with your spirituality either for yourself or with others.

**Spirituality S.M.A.R.T. Goal (Meyer, 2019)**

**What is the Goal?** (Written in the future tense as if already achieved)

_____

_____

**S - Specific.**

What will the goal accomplish?

_____

_____

How and why will it be accomplished?

_____

_____

_____

**M - Measurable.**

How will you measure whether or not the goal has been reached (list at least two indicators)?

_____

_____

_____

**A - Achievable.**

Is it possible?

_____

_____

_____

Have others done it successfully?

_____

_____

_____

Do you have the necessary knowledge, skills, abilities, and resources to accomplish the goal?

_____

_____

_____

Will meeting the goal challenge you without defeating you?

_____

_____

_____

**R - Results-focused.**

What is the reason, purpose, or benefit of accomplishing the goal?

_____

_____

_____

What is the outcome result (not the activities leading up to the result) of the goal?

_____

_____

_____

**T - Time-based.**

What is the established completion date and does that completion date create a practical sense of urgency?

_____

_____

_____

Revised Goal:

_____

## DIVORCE PARTY

Notes:

# Chapter 4
## Health

**Without it does anything else even matter?**

"Health is not valued till sickness comes." Thomas Fuller

"To keep the body in good health is a duty, otherwise we shall not be able to keep our mind strong and clear." Buddha

**What you will get in this chapter**

✓ If I can do it you can do it! 287 pounds to 167 and 6 marathons

✓ REVEALING – my secret - HOW I DID IT!

✓ The Window of Change – comfort / discomfort

✓ The FOOD is just the symptom of something else

✓ I quit smoking 3 packs a day cold turkey and so can you

✓ What is Reality?

✓ Small changes make BIG differences

✓ Motivation – the whip and the carrot

✓ Change happens in an instant and

✓ …my in the PAST eating disorder bulimia

✓ Create your future healthy YOU

**If I can do it you can do it!**

**287 pounds to 167 and 6 marathons**

When I hit rock bottom, as discussed in the Chapter on Spirituality, I had a vision that things would get better. I needed to put my health first; my mind, body, and spirit were depleted. I absolutely knew that for things to improve from where I was to where I wanted them to be, I had to put my health first. I was out of energy and I knew that the road ahead was going to take strength, determination, and persistence.

There were days I would not feel like continuing, moving or even brushing my teeth. I remember looking into the mirror and seeing myself in a place so far from the person I use to be. The clutter in my life seemed so overwhelming, heavy, and felt hopeless. I was so far from where I wanted to be in all areas of my life, and most significantly, my health. It felt like any attempt was not even worth the effort.

Any attempt, seemed like the potential to produce a grain of sand and I needed to produce a whole galaxy of beaches full of sand granules to get to where I wanted to be. I wanted fast and immediate results short term, I was not in the mindset of long term ... yet. It didn't get where I was overnight nor could I get back to where I was, until I began reversing and healing my body back to health. This was not an overnight endeavor.

*When eating an elephant take one bite at a time - Creighton Abrams*

\* \* \* \* \* \*

*The journey of a thousand miles begins with one step - Lao Tzu*

The overwhelming feeling I experienced was from depression and my inaction was analysis paralysis. If you are feeling sad all the time, even if you do not feel like it, reach out and get help. Depression is a serious condition and the best thing you can do is to get outside of yourself instead of isolating yourself. Contact a doctor or friend and talk about it. Get help. Do not wait. As soon as you recognize you are experiencing extended sadness that lingers, get help. Fu%k your ego and pride, get help. Please. Please. Please. There is no reason to suffer alone and to suffer unnecessarily. Get help and feel better!

As the depression was going on, I sought out help with counseling. I recognized feeling stuck with too much to do and I was doing nothing. Analysis paralysis is when you have more than one decision to make at any moment of focusing consciously on what to do. Our mind can't decide two things at the same time. We can only take decisions on one at a time.

Choice is better than no choice. At least we are taking action. And there is no wrong choice. We are surrounded with unlimited resources and sometimes we do not see all the potential we have within us and around us. Whatever happens, we get to learn, grow, and become excellent at making choices by practicing. And even more important, not being paralyzed or stagnant, not moving in any direction. And even not taking action creates a negative inflation. If we were not to move today, we are that much farther behind tomorrow, in 1 year and in 5 years. Even if we get to learn from a choice that sets us back 1 step, it is better to take 1 step back and 5 steps forward than to never do anything, and the never-ending negative economy of not moving at all, and a future that is increasingly growing farther behind than where we potentially could have been.

*Every failure is a lesson.*

*If you are not willing to fail, you are not ready to succeed.*

"There is no failure, only feedback." The only failure is not taking any action. By taking action, we get feedback of what works and what does not work. We grow no matter what the outcome is. By making choices and taking action, we get better, smarter and persist until...

*Where do I even begin or where do I start?* It does not matter so much where you begin, just that you do begin. Start anywhere, if you are not sure where to start, just start from where you are. Search online, go to the library, read a book, join a class, find anyone that has been successful with what you want and ask them how did they do it. Proximity is key! Success leaves clues. Get close to success and it will leave clues to the success you are looking for and how to get it.

My health journey began; I started walking. My first walk was to the mailbox. We lived out in the country in Newtown, Illinois and the mailbox was far enough away, basically at the end of the road, to get a starting walk in. Usually it was worth the convenience of driving to it because of the distance or I would get the mail coming home as it was on the way to my house. However, I decided to pass the convenience and just walk out to it. Feeling comfortable and little by little, I then walked farther distances.

My motivation, hope, and strength grew. I found an apartment, and moved out of that home. It was difficult to finally leave and say goodbye to the house and all the memories. The birthdays, the holidays, this place that meant so much was a hollow shell and the spirit of joy and happiness was gone from that quiet place. Letting it go and to moving forward was the only way.

As things continued to improve with my health, I reached out to my Union and let them know that I wanted to come back to work. Things had dramatically improved in my life. My energy and my spirit were returning. I went back to work and things began to improve financially.

I joined a divorce support group called Divorce Care, a Christian group and program for people going through divorce. I traveled about an hour once a week to attend. The minister who was teaching the course was fighting cancer and he insisted that he continue to teach the program, even though I was the only one attending the group program. I was amazed with his care and determination to continue teaching despite his challenges. It was inspiring that he had a purpose, and teaching this class was important to him.

I continued my walking, going farther then faster, jogging then running. I had been talking about my walking and running on social media, I believe MySpace or Facebook. One day my godbrother (a marathon runner), who had been noticing my posts, encouraged me to think about running a 5k. I said I couldn't do that. He asked me how far I was going now, and I seriously had no idea. I had been running loops around my town in Oakwood, Illinois. I didn't have a clue how far I had been running but just about how long it would take me.

He said measure it! To my surprise, shock, and amazement, I discovered that I was already running a 5k every day or 3.10686 miles. I had this belief that I could never do that! I had a limiting belief. This was limiting my reality and when challenged wasn't, even true or reality. I signed up to run my first 5k in Champaign, Illinois for that 4th of July.

I remember getting passed by a lady pushing a stroller that day and again my negative self-talk would kick in. "Who do you think you are?" "You can't do this." "You will never finish!" And I did go on to finish that race. That was such an incredible moment, doing something I never thought possible.

I continued running; winter, spring, summer, and fall. I ran all the time and accumulated a lot of t-shirts from the 5k's. Then I ran trail runs, then half marathons. Then, within 2 years I successfully completed 6 marathons. Two in Chicago, Illinois, two in Champaign, Illinois, one in Columbus, Ohio and one in Sacramento, California. Sacramento's claim was being the fastest marathon on the planet because it was all downhill. Turns out that running down hill is harder than running flat or uphill unless you trained running downhill because it uses a different muscle group.

My best mile pace was a 6:30 minute mile at a 5k in Watseka, Illinois. My best Marathon time was 3:57 in Chicago, IL. I felt the best I had ever felt in my life. I felt I could do anything. I felt unstoppable. I had thought my life was over, and it nearly was. Now it felt like my life had just begun.

> Yost, Michael J, Chicago, IL,4:52:51, 17780
> Yost, Newton E, Peshtigo, WI,5:05:03, 20468
> Yotz, Christina, Chicago, IL,4:17:39, 9762
> You, David M, Chicago, IL,4:16:43, 9562
> Youhas, David A, Oakwood, IL,3:57:30, 5894
> Youle, Richard, Oxford, GBR,4:05:36, 7340
> Youn, Seijeong, Wilmette, IL,5:56:02, 27991
> Younan, Romana, Chicago, IL,5:00:34, 19596

I had another ah-ha moment, accomplishing something I never thought would happen in my life time. I have been a DJ since 1985, the year I graduated. I was at a middle school with my daughter setting up for the dance and noticed a chin-up bar on stage. I had never done a chin-up, not even close. I was curious to try and then, here comes my negative self-talk. "You're fat, you have always been a fatty, don't even try, you are stupid to think you could even do it."

I thought well, I have accomplished so many things I didn't think were possible, I can at least see how I will do. Maybe this could be my next goal. To my amazement, I could lift myself up effortlessly. I kept on doing chin-ups to about 20. I started to cry. Never, ever in my lifetime, was my absolute belief. Good Lord, what else can I do that I thought was impossible?

**REVEALING** – my secret

**How I Did It**

All my success with weight loss and running in races ... this is awesome! What could possibly be the downside to this health in my life. I kind of felt like a rock star, and I guess in a way I was, considering what I had accomplished and now attracting a lot of attention from people wanting what I had. The only problem I had was explaining it without pissing people off.

I was asked a thousand times "how did you do it?" And I would say exercise more and eat less. It is a simple math equation. It's like accounting. Account for your movement and what you put in your mouth. Move more, eat less.

This was usually met with pursed lips. It was as if I was speaking to them in a condescending way and then they would say, "No really, how did you do it?" At first, I thought they were making a joke. After realizing their sincerity and desperation, eventually I started to be the pissed-off person.

Holy shit, at one point I was running 7 miles a day and 14 on the weekend as a normal routine, like drinking coffee. I found myself judging them, not for not doing what I was doing, but for not doing anything. They would say things like "I can't run a marathon." And then I realized an interesting phenomenon that exists as human nature. We compare ourselves to others and what they are doing or not doing. The solution for someone overweight is not to start running marathons but to begin getting comfortable with discomfort. Not marathon discomfort, but anything more than what they are doing now to cause discomfort. I call this the window of change and comfort /discomfort.

### The Window of Change – comfort / discomfort

I discovered this window of change as I progressed in my running to improve my time and stamina. My body was already healthy with my body and some friends were concerned with my health being too skinny. I was closely monitoring my body fat with a home scale and I was quite safe within the numbers of being healthy with my ratio of body fat.

It was confusing when people who were close to me approached me, saying things like that. At one point I began to question their sincerity or was it that they didn't like me doing so well? I never knew their motives. Someone once told me: "It is none of your business what people think about you." I have learned to say "isn't that interesting" and continue moving on forward.

To improve my running times, I had this incredible thing called the iPod and had it linked with an accelerometer made from a company that rhymes with Bike and a swoosh. The cool thing was that it would give you feedback in your ears. You would set how fast you wanted to run or what is called your 'pace.' If you were too slow, it would say speed up, if you were ahead, it would say good job. After my first time running with it, Neil Armstrong materializes in my head through my ears, and says great job and some motivation bit! Oh my God! I am in love with this thing! It felt like the future! All Star Trek like.

On my next run, I decided to take this pony for a ride and up my pace time. That meant I had to keep up with the lady in my ears or she would scold me. As I began to run and fall behind the pace, "run faster, run faster, run faster" would speak into my ears. I pushed harder than I usually would and was literally getting nauseous from the faster pace. I had to ignore the lady yelling in my ears and slow down. I kept running but at a slower comfortable pace. I was also having thoughts like "You can't do this, you are a failure," familiar negative self-talk.

However, to my amazement, after about 15-30 seconds the sick feeling passed, I regained control over my breathing and I had another burst of adrenaline and felt like running faster. I continued on and would push myself to this upper limit of a faster pace that I grew to know. I could always dip down to a slightly slower pace to regain my breathing, energy, and feeling comfortable with the discomfort of pushing myself harder.

At the upper limit of this window, my mind would freak out and panic, however, I grew to be very comfortable with reaching outside and above what I was capable of. This is the window of change. Stepping just one foot outside of what you are comfortable with to build that confidence and strength. A little discomfort over time then becomes the whole window, shifting and moving to a higher level of performance. And coincidentally, burning a lot of calories.

I am not expecting anyone or you to be where my window was at in that moment. Start somewhere and that is awesome. Maybe your window is walking to the mailbox, around the block, walking your dog, doing some trails at the park or even going to the store and simply putting in distance on your feet. Just jump into the window of change and play with it, wherever you are. Start where you are and move that window of change. The window has dimension variables that you can play with, shifting the window upward and dip into discomfort slightly and return.

The health building variables are Time, Pace, Intensity, and Distance. It is interesting that routine can become boring, so playing games with the variables and challenging yourself to go farther and do more makes it interesting! Measure it and you get to see your success and over time, your progress.

Seeing results, improvement, and feeling better where you are compared to how you use to feel before with less distance, intensity, and time is a BIG motivator and gives you something to celebrate about! These celebrations literally drop dopamine into the pleasure centers of your brain and the feeling of health and exercise is positively addicting.

**Variables**

**Time** – 5 min walk, increase 10, 15, 20, 25, 30 minutes

**Pace** – (faster, speed)

Walk around block 5 minutes, 4, 3, 2, 1 minute!

**Intensity** – Easy, moderate, advanced, challenging)

Vary terrain from easy, challenging to difficult.

Downhill, flat, hills, hiking.

**Distance** – walk around the block 1 time, 2 times, 3 times

It doesn't matter what you do, just do something and measure it!

Get into a peer group for support, motivation, and success. It has been proven that having an accountability person or group almost guarantees success. Sure, you can do it on your own, but what if exercising with others makes it easier, more fun and something you look forward to? It does just that.

There are infinite possibilities. You can join an affordable gym with no maximum days for around $10 a month and you can't afford life without your health. The YMCA will often have group classes where you can get out and meet people that become accountability partners. Online there are Meetup groups for walking and running. The possibilities and opportunities for joining a peer group are infinite.

If you can't find one, start one. I started a walking group online with Facebook and Meetup. People showed up and I was able to talk and walk. Many times, time passed and we were done and I felt so good and was slightly sad we were finished. Time passes fast and you get the workout in.

You can also use online tools like Google Pedometer. https://www.mappedometer.com/ A very cool tool to map out your town or country roads by clicking on the route and it draws on the map with mileage. It has options and variables, again to make it interesting and fun to play with something different, and measure it so you can see the difference you are making in your life.

The simple truth is, do just a little more than you are doing now. This will show you results. Measure your workouts and celebrate your hard work, commitment and resulting success.

**The FOOD is just the symptom of something else**

We are quite the peculiar animals, us human beings. When you really take a close look at us, slow down and really focus on our paradoxical behaviors, it's fascinating. There is scripture in the bible that speaks loudly about our in-decisiveness, our yin and yang, and almost funny human nature that is cast in to every human's DNA.

> *I do not understand what I do. For what I want to do I do not do, but what I hate I do. - Romans 7:15*

I found myself again and again, one evening, standing in front of the refrigerator starring inside at the light, in a daze. I don't even recall how I got there. Maybe I was getting a drink of water from the sink, maybe on my way to the bathroom, but I must have been passing by the refrigerator. I don't know, but there I was, starring into the refrigerator. And as I realized this, I snapped out of the daze and asked myself, how did I get here?

This was not a dream. I was actually awake standing in front of the refrigerator in a sort of a daze, or "trance," a kind of hypnotized state, holding the door open and gazing into the refrigerator. Isn't this interesting. How did I end up standing in front of this freaking refrigerator?

Going back to the scripture on doing what I do not want to do, and not doing what I want to do, almost everyone can identify with this peculiar human condition when it comes to health, exercise, goals, and nutrition. The disturbing thing for me was the realization, that I didn't remember how I got here. I was gazing, in a trance, into the refrigerator, looking into the light, waking up to the awareness of the strangeness of what I was doing.

Consciously awakening and realizing I was standing in front of the refrigerator. Ummmm, was I hungry? Am I in control of my life and my body? I was absolutely caught guilty and holding the evidence, an open door in my hand. What pulled me to materialize and magically awaken consciously in front of the fridge with door open? I don't remember how I got there, standing in front of the fridge, me holding the door open...

Have I lost my mind? Did I have a stroke? Who is driving my fuc%ing bus?

It was the first time I consciously became aware of this bizarre phenomenon that we all experience! WHO IS DRIVING THE BUS? Going back to an earlier story in this chapter about my loosing over 100 pounds and all of the people that were upset, flat out pissed with my results and it felt like they were thinking I was hiding from them the Holy Grail of "How did you do it?" Is this what they were actually seeking? How did I motivate myself? Who is driving the bus of self-control to choose what they put in their mouth or to go to the gym or not? I would eventually uncover the secret to motivation and now I have the answer...

NOW, I can tell you with certainty the answer to the question, who IS driving the bus. You are! Thank you for buying the book, you are finished and now you can close the book and go forward in life having all the answers to all the questions about life and motivation. Thank you. Thank you very much.

OK, OK, OK, I absolutely know the answer and will share it with you in a moment. My quest to find out came from my being so frustrated, slightly hurt, and confused about how upset, pissed, and angry people were with my answer to weight loss... "eat less, exercise more." I discovered the answer during my training in performance coaching, N.L.P. and hypnosis. Initially, I honestly felt this was all 'woo woo' talk, bullshit, but it turns out there is science to back up what I am going to share with you.

I sought out personal development and my earliest readings, well actually listening, were audiobooks of some of the greats: Napoleon Hill,

Jim Rohn, Zig Ziglar, Brian Tracey, Tony Robbins. My first introduction to N.L.P. Neuro Linguistic Programming was from Tony Robbins. I went on to pursue a performance coaching certification also called life coaching (I was never thrilled with that title "life coach") and the science of motivation and human behavior. I went on to pursue N.L.P. and hypnosis. Presently, at the writing of this book, I am a board-certified master hypnotist, board-certified master practitioner in N.L.P. and master practitioner in Time Line Therapy®, master practitioner in vision boards and a relationship coach. I plan to continue on and become a trainer to certify others in this incredibly fascinating field, in N.L.P. and hypnosis.

I love to learn and soak up information like a sponge, and in particular, all the things about our human way of being. In the process, I have learned some incredible scientifically proven facts and practices about how our minds work, how to activate motivation and behavior. And that is what I am going to share with you now.

We have a conscious mind and an unconscious mind. I will use both unconscious and subconscious interchangeably as they are the same thing. Consciously we can only be aware of and focus on 7 sensory things and possibly + or - 2 things, at any moment. Our potential conscious focus is 5 to 9 sensory inputs through what we see, hear, feel, smell and taste. Our unconscious mind is recording and storing everything else from our sensory inputs and taking care of things like breathing, heart rate, blood pressure, regulating body temperature, and everything else that is happening in your body.

The unconscious mind's prime directive is survival. Our unconscious mind will purposefully and unknowingly, sabotage our conscious mind to get what it needs if necessary, this coming from a positive intention to survive. You may consciously want to lose weight, but your subconscious mind trumps your conscious mind, craving for something else. Maybe fulfilling a need to move away from fears, loneliness, boredom, protection, uncomfortable, or anxiety.

The unconscious mind has a primal craving, or a need to survive, but perhaps eating means love to the unconscious mind. That love it felt when eating and being connected with someone significant in your life from the past. And we need love to survive, the unconscious mind wills your body and conscious mind to do what it wants, EVEN BEFORE YOU ARE CONSCIOUSLY AWARE.

It has been scientifically proven that our unconscious mind thinks faster and decides behavior before our conscious mind is aware. Have you ever been driving and a ball, child or deer jumps in front of the car and you jerk the steering wheel and swerve without thinking about it?

Our unconscious mind's prime directive is survival and it will take over physically when it needs to and literally moves your body before you are consciously aware of it. This has been proven in studies where they have hooked up humans to MRI's Magnetic Resonance Imaging and EEGs (Electroencephalography) and have tested and discovered that our unconscious mind activates and decides a response before we are consciously aware of it.

Just like when I found myself gazing into the refrigerator, my physical body moved to where I was standing before that refrigerator, door open and me holding the door, gazing in a trance staring into that fridge. The same things happen with other cravings also like alcohol, coffee, or smoking, although the triggers vary.

**I quit smoking 3 packs a day cold turkey and so can you.**

Years ago, I was a 3-pack-a-day smoker and one day I quit. A similar trance-like state happened just like the refrigerator incident twice after I quit smoking cold turkey. Two weeks after quitting, I drove into a gas station, bought a pack of cigarettes, opened them up, put a cigarette in my mouth AND lit it up, before realizing I quit 2 weeks before. I literally yelled at myself, "what in the hell are you doing?"

This happened one other time a few days later. I know some of you will say it was just a habit and yes, I agree with that, but there's more to it than just that. We want to go just a little deeper into that habit, and also look at what happened just before I unconsciously drove into the gas station on autopilot.

What was the trigger for me that day, that lead to my unconscious mind seeking to have its needs fulfilled? That particular day I had just came from the office, and it was an exceptionally stressful morning. I do not remember exactly what did it, but something triggered me, so that when I left, I automatically headed straight to the gas station.

I responded to the stress with a learned behavior or a "schema" to cope with the stress and fulfill the unconscious mind's need to be met of feeling calm, in control, relaxed. This is important to get to the root cause of the trigger because if we only quit a bad habit, our unconscious mind ABSOLUTELY WILL find another habit that could be worse to have its needs met. If we can recognize the pattern of behavior and see the trigger. If we feel the want to do an undesired behavior, now we have an opportunity to pick a response that we want to do instead and is good for us and over time becomes an automatic healthy response to stress.

What we want to do is to become consciously aware of the trigger and not go to unconscious auto-pilot behavior. This is also called "the drift." People floating around in a trance, in the drift of life, walking around unconsciously on auto-pilot. If we can become mindful of the desire of the unconscious mind needing something, we can then choose something else that fulfills the unconscious mind's need that is healthy for us instead.

We become empowered instead of being affected by what happens in our life, we can be at the cause of our life, by choosing something that supports our health even when things happen that trigger us. This is empowerment. We are not a victim with what life deals us. We recognize that despite a negative event or trigger, we have infinite possibilities and resources to consciously choose from.

We want to write down what is triggering us, and what we want to choose that is a desired response instead. What are your triggers and how would you like to act or do something different instead? Write down your triggers and a new actions.

Trigger Now =    New Healthy Response

_____    _____

_____    _____

_____    _____

_____    _____

_____    _____

**What is reality?**

Reality is a movie we watch through our own eyes and listen to it with our ears and feel it in our body and smell it with our nose and taste it with our tongue. It appears fluid like a movie but it is actually just like a movie made up from a series of continuous snapshots collected through our senses 7 bits (+/- 2 bits) of information at a time (your conscious mind) that is put together like film. Everything from your senses is recorded by your subconscious mind. But what we focus on becomes our conscious reality.

What is mind-blowing is how little what we consciously perceive makes up this awesome, incredible, dynamic, mind blowing action movie we are watching. Only 7 bits of information and potentially plus or minus 2 additional sensory inputs make up our reality. 5 to 9 things we focus on at any moment is our action movie reality. That's it, despite us constantly being bombarded with infinite sensory possibilities! And even more fascinating is that we can choose what we focus on negative or positive and that becomes the movie.

What is the title of the movie of your life presently?

_____

_____

If you could have, be, do anything and money and time were no object how would you like the title of your movie to be called instead?

_____

_____

It is of great value to wisely choose what we focus on because what we focus on expands. What we see, hear, feel, smell, and taste becomes this action movie we are watching, hearing, feeling, smelling and tasting. Our conscious mind learns to do things and skills by consciously doing things. You learned to drive a car perhaps. You had to consciously keep your hands on the steering wheel (1), foot on the brake (2), foot on the gas (3), watch the left mirror (4), watch the rear mirror (5), watch for cars in the right mirror (6), watch the speedometer (7), and now you are already maxed or near maxed at 7 sensory inputs that you can be focused on. Some people or our circumstances allow us to be consciously aware of up to 9 things that we see, hear, feel, smell, and taste. With some people or circumstances, we consciously can only focus and be aware of less than that many sensory inputs.

Now if you are at your maximum of your sensory inputs and you are just learning to drive and hyper-focused on what you are doing, now imagine you are driving through Chicago rush-hour traffic (8), cars are honking (9), and your friend wants to play his favorite 'screamo' music on the radio (10), full blast on the radio and he starts beating the drum beats on your shoulder (11)! Ahhhhhhhhhh! You will definitely begin to have a hard time focusing on driving.

Have you ever said or heard someone say, "turn the radio off, I can't concentrate and drive with that on?" Think about texting and driving or talking on the phone and driving, it is obvious why doing this is so dangerous. People that say they can multi-task is simply not true, an illusion, and a highly ineffective way to be productive and get things done. These same people will confuse being busy with being productive or being successful and they are not the same.

Back to our learning to drive model, after practicing and practicing and practicing how to drive, eventually, at some point, our unconscious mind learns the behavior so well it takes over. We perfect the skill of driving to the point of unconscious learned behavior. We can arrive at home and not remember the drive. This is called driving hypnosis. Think about that, at times we are physically behaving and doing things unconsciously in the world, like driving a 2000-pound vehicle through a labyrinth and somehow we get home safe.

This unconscious learned behavior is something that we want to do and what is REALLY important that I want you to get from this is that the exact same thing is happening when we are doing behaviors that are negative and sabotage ourselves. At one time the self-sabotaging learned behavior was created to survive an event or trauma. The good news is that we can knock out all the legs from the undesired behavior, collapse it and choose something else that we want to do instead.

Why is it that we can only focus on 7 +/-2 sensory inputs? We evolved and survived to not be too scatter-brained to miss what is important. We would go insane if our minds took in everything, and would not have been able to survive as a species. We would be so scattered-brained we would not be able to accomplish anything.

Have you ever been in a noisy room, and across the room someone speaks to you and you hear them? Out of all that other noise, you recognize that voice speaking to you. Think about how incredible that actually is and how we just take that for granted. How amazing our mind is to delete all of the other sound and yet consciously allow you to focus only only hearing them. Our mind will do some other tricks to get us on the 7 +/- 2 focus, besides deleting information like sound. It will also distort perception and generalize information.

Make no mistake, we are over-bombarded with stimulus from TV, radio, phones, and billboards now more than ever. Everyone is competing and marketing for our attention, to capture that sliver of consciousness, that 7 +/- 2 pieces of your focus. All this as well as the rest of your mind that is unconsciously recording everything whether you are consciously aware of it or not.

Not only are we marketed to in ways you would consciously understand, but we are also receiving covert triggers from other negative marketing, and gloom and doom media that activates our fight/flight response, that primes our unconscious mind to respond, feel, and behave differently than we would if we were not experiencing fear. There is good reason to limit yourself from media and media devices. Bad news is just a form of priming the mind to take action and a marketing strategy to capture your conscious real estate. Fear captures our attention and activates our sympathetic nervous system or fight/freeze/flight response. You have heard it said before, people that do not watch the news are happier and feel more at peace. Consequently, we make better, rational decisions that support our success, when we are in a state of abundance and not scarcity and fear.

### Small changes make BIG differences

I have a friend from grade school that lost over 100 pounds and he became a runner. And of course, I had to ask him, how did he do it? He had a beautiful and simple answer. He didn't really talk about it on social media. I had actually noticed his transformation and was just about to ask him if he had lost a large amount of weight, when he announced on Facebook one day that he did lose a lot of weight.

His response to how he did it was simple and it really made sense. I actually felt, his success was something doable for anyone. Want to know his secret? He said small changes every week. There is some research behind this that setting smaller goals are more likely to be successful. Think about it, make a goal so small that you absolutely can achieve it.

He stopped drinking soda and started drinking water instead 1 week. I have heard so many people repeatably do this alone, and over a couple of months successfully lost 30-40 pounds. It makes sense, right?

Add up all that sugar in calories, not to mention the horrible effects it has on the body, add it up and over time a little bit adds up to a lot of fat. Imagine 30 pounds of bacon on a plate. That's a lot of bacon.

This same technique can be used for food and exercise. Just add one thing different each week consistently. Start walking around the block 3-5 days a week. It gets your heart rate up, metabolism up, tones and strengthens your muscles, brings oxygen to your brain, and creates a dopamine release in your brain to feel fabulous. Just one thing over time adds up to big results!

Add more green vegetables to your meals. It physically fills you up, sustains that full-feeling full longer, nourishes your entire body with vitamins and minerals, scrubs your intestines and colon clean, and as they say, if your poop isn't floating eat more greens! And it will. Apparently, more than your body gets lighter, the healthier you become.

Start to meditate in the mornings for 5-20 minutes. Sit in stillness, without distraction, and notice all the bullshit you can't let go of. No matter how hard you try not to think about anything, the stuff that is bothering you will surface. Do not resist or it will persist. Focus on your breathing, take deep breaths in and let it out twice as slow. Focus only on your breathing and the stillness.

If you hear a car drive by, think a simple word, "car" and release the thought as you breathe out. Continue focusing on your breathing. Meditation is like a muscle and the more you focus on your breathing, the less thought you will have. Just be yourself in a peaceful state of being. Overtime you will discover that all you need in any moment is just to breathe, everything else can wait.

One week stop eating fries if you eat fries. Fries are starchy, high carbohydrate, high glycemic, fried, and are just crap to your body and have no health value. We want to enjoy food, nourish our body, and feel good. Fries will cause an insulin spike followed by a lethargic crash. Try possibly replacing fries with a fruit.

For one week record everything you eat and count the calories. If you can't measure it, you can't manage it. There are so many cool smart phone apps that make it easy to track your nutrition, including bar code scanner options that simplify and speed up the process to record food. Keeping it simple will make it successful. Set small goals that you absolutely can achieve and feels doable.

## Motivation – the whip and the carrot

We are motivated by two things, the carrot and the whip. The challenge with motivation by the whip (which is very effective short term) is that long term, we no longer feel the whip when we get closer to a goal. For example, if you want to lose weight because you don't like feeling tired, after you lose the weight and feel awesome, you no longer feel the whip. The whip is not a motivator any more.

Going back to the "what you focus on expands" principle. Focus on the VALUE of what losing weight gives you. Motivate yourself with the carrot. This simple shift in thinking makes all the difference in creating powerful outcomes. This motivation sets you up for success in the future by creating a powerful magnetic pull toward what you want. When you are not getting what you want, your unconscious motivation kicks in to do whatever it takes to maintain, what you focus on. You are continually pulled toward what you want.

Like a beacon that you are moving toward, when you get off track you know because you are moving away from the light and intensity. The source of the light gives you direction to calibrate which way to move to take you toward the light.

**Change happens in an instant and ... my prior eating disorder**

At one time I hated food. I had no enjoyment and I associated food with pain. I didn't think I had a problem. It was something I had been doing from about the age of 8 to the age of 40. It was a dangerous way of me coping with stress and negative feelings and avoiding making new choices that made me anxious and fearful.

When significant stress was going on in my life, I would go into a tiring cycle of bulimia. Eating huge amounts of food, then forcing myself to vomit. Then repeat this cycle over and over again to exhaustion while lying on the bathroom floor hanging over a toilet. The bulimia would usually numb my feelings, but not always or completely but enough to shift my state of mind.

I now have easy and powerful tools that I discovered in my N.L.P. training that shift my state of mind, anytime, anywhere, in an instant. I can easily and often automatically shifting a negative state of mind to a positive resourceful state of mind. It's easy to focus on what you do not want. Instead, flip it.

What is it that you want instead? Begin to focus on that desire for what you want instead. How do you want to feel instead? Think of a time that you felt that way. Go back in your mind and see that experience. How does it feel to feel like that? And now, like magic, you begin to feel that state of mind, you begin to notice your own present state of mind shifting to that positive state. Make that feeling twice as strong. Feel that feeling twice as strong in your body now. Now, double it again. Continue feeling that growing feeling spread throughout your entire body. It's that easy. Piece of cake!

Back to my eating disorder. I was excellent at hiding it, as far as I know. Except for the inquisitive and occasional "where did all the food go"? It was my choice of self-medication. Some choose drugs, alcohol, smoking, or risky self-sabotaging behavior in various forms, I chose bulimia. Bulimia is a serious eating disorder, marked by binging on food followed by purging, throwing the food up, or other methods to avoid weight gain. I did not enjoy food.

I had been going to a counselor related to an entirely different event. During one of our sessions I happened to mention this thing I had been doing. Interestingly and surprising to me, this became the main focus. I was actually annoyed because it didn't seem as significant for my main reason for seeing the counselor for an issue.

This became the main focus of counseling visits. They tried many challenging reframes. A reframe is a technique that challenges your belief system through conversation and getting someone to examine what they believe and is it really true. Is it true all the time?

Humans process their experiences differently, applying meaning to their individual experiences or interactions. You could say we are meaning making machines. When we take in life and what happens to us, the information 7 +/- 2 pieces of sensory information we make up a meaning of the experience and everyone associates a different meaning to their experience. We make up the meaning of life. If we can make up that we are in a negative state of mind, we can then also choose to make up a positive meaning. Regardless of what is happening in the world, we make up the meaning of our life. A swastika is a symbol meaning horror and despair to one person and means a religious symbol and love to another person. We make the meaning of our experiences. Wouldn't it be of great value to choose the meaning?

Additionally, everyone uniquely selects what 7 +/- 2 pieces of information they allow into their focus. It's possible for us to limit what we focus on and distort that reality. On that same note, we can generalize the meaning or focus on the negative, deleting all the positive attributes; believing only bad things are happening around us, standing knee-deep in things to be grateful for or find resources we could use to climb out of the dark hole of scarcity.

Our beliefs are all made up, we are not born with them, they are learned, they are flexible and can change. We take our beliefs to be true as sure as gravity is real and otherwise assume their truths, even when they are false truths. It's worth critically thinking and challenging our beliefs, and are they our beliefs or someone else's beliefs? Is the world flat? Do we actually know that is true or did someone tell us that?

The counselor continued challenging my thinking. They inquired about potential complications including acid reflux and ulcers to esophageal cancer. I had a reasoning for all of that and why that would not happen. I diluted the food of choice with milk and the acid would interact with the milk and curdle it and lesson the acids erosive strength. I believed it was harmless, the result was curdled milk and no discomfort or acidity.

**Change happens in an instant!**

This went on for some time and they continued for days with new reasons that I would refute, until one day they asked me, "Did you know that people with bulimia, statistically gain weight when they are in that phase of binge purge?" This caught my attention. I started thinking about it and it was absolutely true, I would actually gain a lot of weight during those times. I remember laughing at myself. She's right! And what I thought was the payoff was a fraud.

*Change happens in an instant, when our belief system changes.*

Think of the implications of this in the context that food is the symptom. It's not the food causing the weight. When we get to the root of the symptom, the trigger of the symptom, uncover the need that the unconscious mind is seeking out AND WILL ABSOLUTELY FIND A WAY TO GET IT, we consciously have this beautiful opportunity to change and choose something different instead.

Choose something that meets both the need of our unconscious mind and the need for health. I chose to walk the weight off that was holding me back. The drive was so exponentially freaking ridiculously powerful, automatically I was powerfully DRIVEN to lose over 100 pounds and run 6 marathons in 2 years. And in all honesty, it felt effortless. I didn't understand it then but I do now. My transformation is absolute testimony to how powerful our unconscious mind is when we get in alignment with it and working for us. I had never done anything like this in my entire life. An anomaly in its purest form. And to me it was a miracle.

That day was the end of my bulimia. Over 30 years my 'routine' changed immediately in that instant. It has never reoccurred nor any desire to do so. What does this mean for you? We resist the simplicity of change. This work is easier than you knew before. It is fascinating that change can happen in an instant! This has to do with our beliefs and values. Getting our unconscious mind's needs fulfilled frees up space to design our future, transform our lives, and step into our future self successfully.

### Create your future and healthy YOU

The purpose of these exercises is to get your unconscious aligned with your conscious. What is the purpose of health? What does your health look like, sound like, and feel like to you? If goals in any area of your life are challenging to accomplish, these exercises are truly magic.

By starting with purpose, we create an automatic pull toward that purpose on an unconscious level. Don't think of a pink elephant and automatically you can't not think of a pink elephant. Let's focus on what you want out of health now and start moving toward it now. It's that easy.

**On a scale of 0-10 how important is this change for you?**

0 being not important at all, 5 neutral and 10 very important.

0  1  2  3  4  5  6  7  8  9  10

Whatever you chose, what would it take for you to be committed to increase that number slightly up 1 or 2 numbers?

_____

_____

**On a scale of 0-10 how confident are you that this change is possible?** 0 being not important at all, 5 neutral and 10 very important.

0  1  2  3  4  5  6  7  8  9  10

Whatever you chose, what would it take for you to be committed to increase that number slightly up 1 or 2 numbers?

_____

_____

Why is health important to you and how do you value health?

_____

_____

What would it be like if health is important to you?

_____

_____

What would it be like if health is not important to you?

_____

What is the pay-off of good health, what do you get out of it?

_____

_____

How do you know you have good health? How do you feel when health is excellent?

_____

_____

Go back to a time when you felt your most healthy, what do you see, what do you hear, what do you feel?

_____

_____

How do other experience you when your health is excellent?

_____

_____

See yourself in the future, already having accomplished this health goal. What do you see, what do you hear, how do you feel?

_____

_____

**Design Your Health Plan – Mind, Body and Spirit.**

## Health S.M.A.R.T. Goal (Meyer, 2019)

**What is the Goal?** (Written in the future tense as if already achieved)

_____

_____

_____

### S - Specific.

What will the goal accomplish?

_____

_____

_____

How and why will it be accomplished?

_____

_____

_____

### M - Measurable.

How will you measure whether or not the goal has been reached (list at least two indicators)?

_____

_____

_____

**A - Achievable.**

Is it possible?

_____
_____
_____

Have others done it successfully?

_____
_____
_____

Do you have the necessary knowledge, skills, abilities, and resources to accomplish the goal?

_____
_____
_____

Will meeting the goal challenge you without defeating you?

_____
_____
_____

**R - Results-focused.**

What is the reason, purpose, or benefit of accomplishing the goal?

_____
_____

What is the outcome result (not the activities leading up to the result) of the goal?

_____
_____
_____

**T - Time-based.**

What is the established completion date and does that completion date create a practical sense of urgency?

_____
_____
_____

Revised Goal:

_____
_____
_____
_____

Notes:

_____
_____
_____

# Chapter 5
## Relationships

**Self, Family, Romance, Community**

"Forgiveness is giving up on the hope of ever having a better past."

"No man is an island entire of itself; every man is a piece of the continent, a part of the main; if a clod be washed away by the sea, Europe is the less, as well as if a promontory were, as well as any manner of thy friends or of thine own were; any man's death diminishes me, because I am involved in mankind. And therefore, never send to know for whom the bell tolls; it tolls for thee."

"We all deserve to be happy"

"Feel like a bad parent? The Australian Quokka, toss their babies at predators so they can escape."

**What you will get in this chapter**

✓ Work on your inner world to change your outer world

✓ Though shalt feel bad – dealing with shame and guilt

✓ YOU are not your past

✓ What is the value of the past?

✓ Dreaded Drama Triangle – victim, persecutor, rescuer

✓ Human needs – Maslow's hierarchy of needs

✓ Toxic Relationships, Addictions, and Potholes...

✓ Using NLP and Relationships – Building rapport

✓ The foundation of communication – Rapport

✓ 3 elements that make all relationships successful

✓ Building Trust in self and others

✓ Releasing Negative Emotion

✓ We all deserve to be happy (:

✓ Conflict Resolution Template

**Work on your inner world to change your outer world**

If you don't like your circumstances or anything outside of you, work on your inner game. Our outer world is only a reflection of us internally. If you look out into the world and see anger, people you can't trust, people that do not keep their commitments, you are looking in a mirror, pointing at yourself and pronouncing GUILTY! I realize this blows your mind if you have never considered the possibility that what you see outside of yourself is only a reflection of what you see inside of yourself.

Just for fun, let us consider the implications of what this means and how it impacts you, whether you accept the idea or not accept the idea. If it is true, then also all the good you see in the world is a reflection of the good you see in yourself. We can choose what we are looking for outside of us and fascinatingly, we then attract more of that good in our life.

As discussed in the chapter on Health, we can on perceive 7 +/- 2 pieces of sensory information at any one time. There are infinite possible things to focus on all around us constantly. If you are sitting, you now feel the weight of your bottom on the chair or you notice the weight of your body pushing down on the floor. You were not focusing on it before until I drew your focus to it. It is the same thing with all you see in the world.

What you focus on expands. If you see bad in the world, it is because out of everything in the world outside of yourself, good and bad, you notice bad. Isn't that interesting? This is human nature. Good and bad is outside of us all, and what we see, hear and feel outside of us, is a reflection of our inner world. We see outside of us what we see, hear, feel, and experience, inside of us, by what we choose to focus on.

STOP and listen, this is IMPORTANT! This does not mean you are not a good person. It only represents your internal representation in a single moment in time. Don't go to that place of shame. "Oh my God, the world is right, I am a bad person" NOT TRUE because you are made up of infinite love and good inside you. And you SEE, HEAR, AND FEEL that in the world when you see, hear, and feel that in yourself!

If you are not happy with your present circumstances and the world around you, START with your inner world. Love yourself first, and that is not being selfish. Love yourself first so that you can reflect that joy, happiness, love, and light into the world. Be a beacon of love and that love will return to you, reflect back to you and warm, light up, and care for you.

I want to invite you to close your eyes and use your imagination. Look into the future and see yourself surrounded by people that love you and that you love. How do those relationships look in your life? What are you experiencing? How does it feel and what does it mean to you, having these relationships? How does that fulfill you? What is their significance and value in your life? What does it look like, sound like, and feel like?

_____

_____

_____

_____

_____

## Though shalt feel bad – dealing with shame and guilt

No matter how overwhelming, horrible, despairing and painful my divorce was, nothing hurt worse than seeing my children go through the divorce too. Turns out that kids are incredibly resilient. Thank goodness for that!

My children have all turned out to be wonderful kids. I am proud of and love them all. Now they are adults and I love how uniquely beautiful they are as individuals and who they have become and continue to grow on their journey. Things have significantly changed for the better, for us all, and yet the impact of the past haunts me to this day, now and then, briefly, when I choose to let it.

Every now and then I will see in my children's eyes, a reflection into that past painful time. Instead of focusing on ALL the POSITIVE things in the present, I go down that rabbit hole. Then feeling how sad I felt about that reality that I took them through, until I catch myself, as I have trained myself to snap out of it, as I will show you how to move forward. It is easy when you consciously become aware that there is a feeling that you want to feel instead.

I'm still a work in progress, as are we all. I continue to work on letting go of the toxic past, learn the lesson, and let it go; release it. I free myself to accept good things and relationships. I cherish, give thanks, appreciate, and have gratitude for the positive and awesome moments and people in my life.

What do you get out of holding onto the past? Being right or wrong? Being a martyr or a victim? Is it challenging to let go of the past because someone else wants to hold onto the past? With every challenge you face, what is the lesson that you are thankful for, moving forward?

There is very little value in the past that we can't change. We can only influence our future with choices we make in the moment of NOW. Now is what is happening and now is the only control we have in our lives and our future destinations. Starting with the choices we make now, will set a new path to a better future.

I want you to record this in your brain and remember it. I don't mean to seem heartless or cold with what I am saying about letting the past go or not being able to change the past. The facts are clear, we can't change the fucki%g past. Retain the lesson and move forward with that knowledge and let the past flow past and let it go!

Past event: _____

Lesson learned: _____

Past event: _____

Lesson learned: _____

Past event: _____

Lesson learned: _____

Past event: _____

Lesson learned: _____

Past event: _____

Lesson learned: _____

Past event: _____

Lesson learned: _____

Past event: _____

Lesson learned: _____

Past event: _____

Lesson learned: _____

Past event: _____

Lesson learned: _____

## Now let it go!

**YOU are not your past**

Listen close. Holding on to the past use to trap you into not moving forward, growing, healing toward a brighter future for you, your children, friends, family, coworkers, basically the world. The past can potentially fool us into believing we are our past, which is bullshit. In any moment we can make a new choice in our lives that sets a new path and a new direction and destination in our lives. We are full of infinite potential in our choices right now and for the future.

You were kind of being a selfish asshole dwelling in the past, by forcing yourself, your children, and everyone around you to suffer about something that is not even real. Yes, it happened, yes it was real then, and now it really is in the past.

You may have a picture or movie you keep replaying in your mind. You may see it, hear it, and feel it. And yes it use to be sad or even traumatic. But it's not you now and it's not real. It's just an old obsolete movie that was recorded then and you replay it sometimes.

### What is the value of the past?

The value of the past is the lesson that something did or did not work, and holding appreciation and gratitude for the wisdom you now have from it. Yes, it is worth a brief reflection contemplating. What other resources and choices were there or available to you at the time that you did not see? We make the best choices available to us in any given moment, although there were other choices and resources available to us. We can become blinded to our abundance and infinite possibilities, by what we choose to focus on and see / hear / feel in the limited 7 +/- 2 sensory inputs.

It has been said that if you want to be successful, get really good at failing. This statement seems ridiculous at first, yet it reveals a truth about success. The only way to improve is to keep trying. At first, we really suck at something new. It is only by doing something poorly that we become excellent at it.

A baby learning to walk does not give up and as a parent we do not look at them as a failure. Take action and try until you get the result you want. And the past is a success no matter what happens, and is something to celebrate when we look at, we tried! We took action. There is no other way to reach goals other than taking action. Anyone who has been successful has a past full of failure!

If you are upset with the baby who was not successful at their first attempt at walking, forgive that baby! It is not what happens to you, but what you do next that matters. If you have fallen down in past attempts, pick yourself back up and try again, and try again and again and again. Persist until you succeed.

## Dreaded Drama Triangle – victim, persecutor, rescuer

Continuing working on our inner world so that we can powerfully transform our outer world, I want to introduce you to a fascinating model that is so obvious and fascinating to observe all around you. This is a game that is played at work, relationships, and even between pets and humans. A toxic game that is being played out every day that you can decide to powerfully shift your role from powerless to powerful.

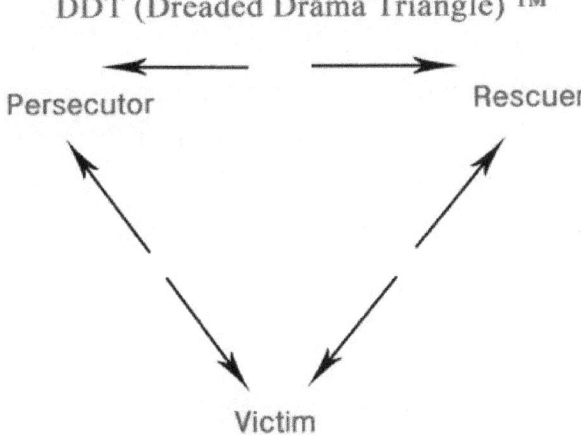

The D.D.R. Dreaded Drama Triangle concept was first developed and noted by a Stephen Karpman (Stephen B. Karpman, 1968) in 1968 a well respected psychologist. This comes from the psychology association with Transactional Analysis. Later, David Emerald (Emerald, 2014) expanded on Stephen's original work. He came up with the acronym D.D.T. Dreaded Drama Triangle and wrote about it in his book: The Power of T.E.D. The Empowerment Dynamic. David contacted Stephen Karpman who acknowledged David's work as a powerful way to transform the triangle to empowerment and even wrote a forward in David's book.

DDT is a game that people play with a group of people with at least 2 people. The aim of the game is to handoff your negative feeling to someone else. There is always an instigator, persecutor, and a rescuer.

Let us take a look at the D.D.T. and how it can impact relationships. Do you recognize any of the roles?

<u>Victim</u> – the person that feels hopeless and powerless, this always happens to me. They do not feel in control and they are anticipating the other shoe to drop.

<u>Rescuer</u> – takes responsibility for another person's problems, they see someone else's problem, take ownership and makes it their problem, they do not look at their own lives, that could be a total mess. Look at that poor soul, I am nice, I can help them! If they would only listen to what I am saying, they would be successful and happy.

<u>Persecutor</u> – they are the bully, I'm right, they are wrong, self-righteousness, they deserve that.

We can be in any of these roles and can move around and be all the roles. We usually have a favorite, or a tendency to start at one and move to another. All three of these roles are disempowering and the relationships between them are not healthy relationships. So how do we get out of the drama triangle?

**Transform your role to empowerment**

TED (The Empowerment Dynamic) ™

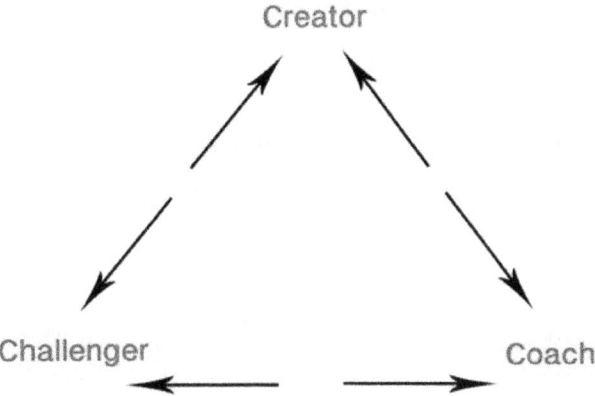

**Victim** – if you are the victim, you want to become the survivor. What am I grateful for in my life? What are the good things already happening in your life that you appreciate?

**Rescuer** – if you are the rescuer, become a coach or a teacher. Ask what do you think you can do to get a different outcome? What is it that you want instead? Instead of jumping in and trying to fix them, set boundaries on what you will do and how much time you have to listen, encourage, and support them.

**Persecutor** - if you are the persecutor, you want to become the challenger. Recognize this is not your problem and you do not have to fix it. You can only control your choices and not the choices of others.

I want to encourage you to further your study into the DDT model including reading the book by "The Power of T.E.D. The Empowerment Dynamic" – https://powerofted.com/. Change your inner world and this will change your outer world automatically.

## Human needs –

## Maslow's hierarchy of needs

There is a theory commonly known in the world of psychology that predicts our happiness. Going through a divorce, well ... will cause the dynamics to get all jacked up. There are many tools and lenses to look through that can create a shift of thinking or a glimpse of understanding. Maslow's theory has continued to be a powerful tool to look at where we are suffering and see where we want to be instead. "To Know Thyself" and where we hurt comes just before what is on the other side, knowing how you want to feel instead. What's interesting with Maslow's law is that it recognizes a progression from one level to the next. We can't be happy in any other area of our life until the previous level is met.

Maslow's hierarchy of needs is a theory proposed by Abraham Maslow in his 1943 paper "A Theory of Human Motivation" in Psychological Review. Maslow subsequently extended the idea to include his observations of the humans' innate curiosity of humans.

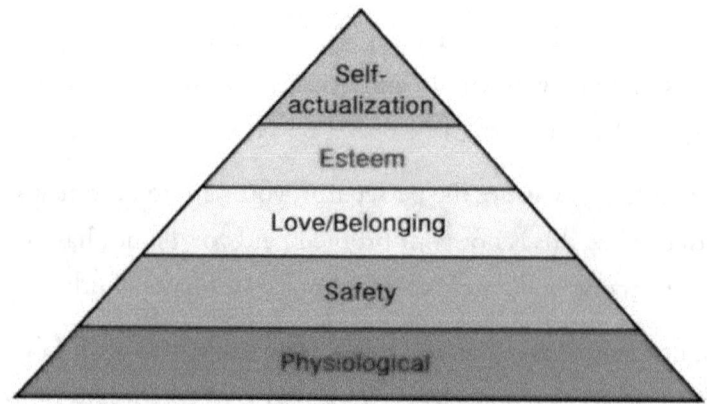

Our hierarchy of needs begins at the foundation of the triangle and goes upward. The first level is physiological - relating to the branch of biology that deals with the normal functions of living organisms and their parts. This must be met first. Once the physiological need is met, then we can work on the next level, safety. None of the other needs above can be met, until the need for safety is met AND all the other needs below are maintained.

Next on the hierarchy of needs is love and belonging and that brings us to this chapter on relationships. How is your physiology? Our mind and body are connected. It is a scientific fact that prolonged or severe emotional stress can affect a person's physical body. Good and bad. Thoughts are things and produce chemicals from pleasure to flight or fight. If our thoughts are fear we produce adrenaline and cortisol that can long term lead to producing physiological effects that may need an intervention, or lead to the need of medical treatment.

We can't resolve an issue in our life at the level it exists. If relationships in our lives are challenged or lacking, it is that we have to look below that level to make sure that we meet those needs first. How is the need for safety in your life being met? How do you know when you are safe? Where is safety working already in your life? Where have the challenges with safety been and how can you create feeling safer now?

**Toxic Relationships, Addictions, and Potholes ...**

We become like the 5 people we hang around with the most. Maybe it's time to upgrade who you spend time with? Challenge yourself to become more than who you are now. Why not choose excellent people to be around? Why not ask where do I want to grow in my life and find the people who are already doing that?

Through my divorce I discovered that some people in my life were toxic people, some close friends. They didn't have my best interests in mind. Surround yourself with people that inspire you to rise up and be like them. Surround yourself with people that leave you feeling good. Align yourself with people that share your same values.

During my time with the counselor that worked with me on my bulimia, some time was spent in an addictions support group. I was surrounded by others who were all trying to self-medicate their problems and working through challenges. Drugs, alcohol, food, sex, self-mutilation, and even relationships can be addictive. This is a poem that is often shared in the addiction community. Simple yet powerful for letting something go that we think we control yet do not.

### *Autobiography in Five Chapters - by Portia Nelson (1920 -2001)*

### *Chapter One*

I walk down the street.

There is a deep hole in the sidewalk.

I fall in.

I am lost .... I am helpless.

It isn't my fault.

It takes forever to find a way out.

### *Chapter Two*

I walk down the street.

There is a deep hole in the sidewalk.

I pretend that I don't see it.

I fall in again.

I can't believe I am in this same place.

But, it isn't my fault.

It still takes a long time to get out.

### Chapter Three

I walk down the same street.

There is a deep hole in the sidewalk.

I see it is there.

I still fall in ... it's a habit ... but, my eyes are open.

I know where I am.

It is my fault.

I get out immediately.

### Chapter Four

I walk down the same street.

There is a deep hole in the sidewalk.

I walk around it.

### Chapter Five

I walk down another street.

## Using NLP with Relationships

What is the only thing we control in this world? We only control our own choices. We do not control others' choices but we can potentially influence them. And there is good reason to want to do that in a positive way. We want to be able to let a friend or our kids know that the path they are on will lead them to a place they do not want to go. We want to influence a co-worker or employee that their action will result in their termination. We want to influence a friend in an abusive relationship that cannot see that they are not loving themselves and allowing someone else to hurt them.

## The foundation of communication

### – Rapport

We can't influence anyone including ourselves without creating and maintaining relationships and all relationships start with communication. For communication to be effective, we must first start with building rapport, the invisible glue of relationships. Rapport allows us to speak into someone's listening. If you do not have rapport, you will definitely know it. Communications will be like speaking to a brick wall.

How do you create a rapport with someone? Do you have to maintain rapport? What if someone is resisting my communication and how do I establish this rapport? Rapport is actually easy to do and maintain when we understand what it is, how we work toward it, and we intentionally set out to do it. Here's how it works...

I'm a father of four children in their 20s and a certified relationship coach. Additionally, I'm a master hypnotist, a master practitioner in time line therapy®, and NLP and a performance coach. I'll be introducing you now to using NLP to improve your family relationships and all relationships for that matter.

NLP stands for neuro linguistic programming. NLP, in simple terms, is the study of excellence. Its origins go back to the 1970s, created by Richard Bandler, a psychology student at UC Santa Cruz and Dr. John Grinder, an associate professor of linguistics. Bandler modeled the methods of Virginia Satire and Pearl Fritz, who were extraordinarily effective therapists of their time as well as many others. But he created the process, drawing from the excellence in others that can be modeled and replicated with incredible effectiveness.

If someone has done something successful, so can you by modeling them. Their original intention was to study the principles that governed the language structure and define the techniques and skills used by successful therapists. What they learned became and continues to evolve into NLP.

Neuro Linguistic Programming. N is for neuro - from the brain and neurology. L is for linguistics - from language and communication. P is for programming - from our fascinating behavior patterns and strategies that we consciously and unconsciously run. How we want to utilize NLP with relationships is around our language, tonality, and body language to communicate effectively.

NLP is a powerful communication tool with others and with ourselves. Through our five senses we see, hear, feel, taste, and smell the world. Primarily we experience it through VAK - visual, auditory, and kinesthetic, or feelings. We also individually have a dominant sense. Sixty percent of people are visually dominant, 20 percent are auditory, and 20 percent are kinesthetic.

Additionally, there are sub-modalities to our senses. Bright or dim, loud or soft, sad or happy, sweet or sour. For now, the main thing I want you to focus on is to discover the primary modality for yourself and for others by identifying and matching the primary modalities. This will take you leaps and bounds in your relationships by building rapport.

And it's easy to find out. Just listen to the words being used to describe the world around you, and you will HEAR it in their language, and you will know it when you SEE it, and you will just get a FEELING that you have discovered it. People will communicate using sensory descriptive words like see, hear, or feel and that will indicate their primary sense they use in the world. We want to talk and match people in their dominant language to build rapport.

Here are three simple tips to use and help you to improve your family relationships as well as any relationship.

Tip number one - build rapport. Have you ever experienced resistance in a relationship or even yourself resisting something? Whenever there is a breakdown in a relationship, go back to building rapport. Rapport is fundamental and the foundation of all working relationships and communication. Resistance, is only the lack of rapport. Here is a simple technique to get in rapport with someone. Match and mirror someone's body language, tonality, and words.

People that are like each other, like each other. It is absolutely a must that you do it with integrity and with a clear intent that you want to be in rapport with someone because you care for the relationship. Match their body language, match their voice tonality, match their language using words that are in their dominant sense. Visual, auditory or kinesthetic.

### 3 elements that make- ALL relationships successful

Tip Number two - maintain working relationships by being aware of three key elements that are always present in every relationship. ***Communication, Commitment, and Trust.*** Here's how it works.

Relationship element number one - COMMUNICATION. We just explained rapport and it is the foundation of communication. If you don't have rapport, you don't have effective communication. Always start with rapport to communicate with your kids, your spouse, or significant other. With communication, 55 % is unspoken use in body language, 38 % is unspoken use in tonality. Only 7 % of communication is spoken using words. This is why texts and emails get us into trouble.

Having a phone conversation is better than a text or email because voice tonality can be heard but is still not as effective as communicating in person. If it is an important conversation, communicate in person.

Relationship element number two - COMMITMENTS. In a relationship, we make promises and commitments. I will take out the trash. I will give you lunch money. I will do the dishes. I will meet you at our favorite restaurant at 7 p.m. Friday night for our anniversary dinner.

### Building Trust in self and others

Relationship element number three – TRUST. We either keep our promise and commitments or we break them. And that then impacts the third element in Relationships – TRUST. We either are building or tearing down trust. Trust is easy to break. If we don't keep our commitments there is a lot of work to rebuild it, versus keeping commitments.

Trust absolutely can be rebuilt. Always go back to building rapport, communicating clear commitments. Maintain and keep your commitments with integrity, and this builds strong trust and healthy relationships. And most important, the ability to speak into others' listening even when it is tough love and painful.

Tip Number three. The last tip using NLP is for relationships, unsticking people, and relationships from the past. I literally interrupt people and say moving forward … This helps move others to a working future. When family relationships are in breakdown mode, it is because of something that happened in the past. Sometimes we just want that other person to play their part in the relationship as we think they should. Maybe even generate expectations without clearly defined commitments being made.

When we confront the other person on the offense, they can go into a story or the drift of the reasons why they broke a commitment. They are not being accountable for the choices they made, that were the direct cause of the outcome they got.

My dog ate my homework. I was talking to my boss and I didn't pay the parking meter. And that's why I got my car towed. First of all, before we start to go and call people out on accountability, it is worth a serious self-check. How are we with our own integrity and the commitments we make? To ourselves and others, when no one is watching? We want to be impeccable with our own word. Remember that timber in our own eye as we complain about a spec of sand some other persons eye. Let us first be the example of integrity to those we allow in our life and close to us, then others around us will allow us to value and expect integrity in them.

The only thing we control in this world are our choices. I'll repeat that because it's that important. The only thing we control in this world is our choices. We do not control others' choices. Therefore, our best chance at influence over others is being impeccable with our word. Keeping our commitments and building deep and strong trust. And we have to walk the talk.

We teach others how to treat us by how we treat each other and what we allow. When a relationship is in breakdown and not working, I always start with building rapport, even if I do not feel like it. It is easier to maintain a relationship as they are happening, instead of avoiding and being overgrown with weeds from lack of rapport, broken promises, not calling people on accountability and trusts not being rebuilt.

Sometimes being accountable can feel like a hot seat but it doesn't need to be. Accountability, it's simply accounting for the choices made, without judgment of others and of self and this can build rapport. Otherwise it can sound like excuses and that can break trust.

Here are three suggestions to move forward. Number one -clearly state and discuss the commitment that was broken, what was expected and what happened instead. Number two - avoid the story or the drift. This can be a huge time waster, an emotional vampire, and be counterproductive, and flat out ineffective waste of time.

We cannot change the past, and dwelling there does not have value. What other choices could you have made or resources were there that you could have used to support you?

Number three - here is the important part that is usually missed. The language of moving forward. When we call people on their stuff, don't leave them there trapped in the past being expressed through our language. We don't want to potentially convince people they are their past because no one is their past.

In any moment we all have the possibility and ability to make new choices in the present moment and set a new path moving forward in an entirely new direction with an entirely new outcome. People don't want to hear, they are incompetent or ignorant, distrustful, afraid, stupid, ruining their life, or unreliable.

They can go from guilt to shame or from thinking to knowing they are that. They are future pacing themselves or hypnotizing themselves to who they see themselves to be. We want to move them forward in their vision, hearing and feeling. How they see, hear and feel themselves in a successful future.

Humans have a physical concept of time associated with the position of their body. As well as, a direction in relationship to their body from past, to the future also called a timeline. If I was to ask you to close your eyes and think about a past event, can you point to it? If I was also to ask you with your eyes still closed to think about a future event, can you point to it? Now if you were to draw a line from the past location to the present and to the future location this is your timeline. It is fascinating that we have a physical and directional representation in relation to our body and in relationship to memories that have happened and have not yet happened.

How we think about time, and talk about time to ourselves and others, and what tense of time affects us. We don't want to leave people trapped in the past in our relationships and shortcomings. We want to acknowledge and resolve the past. Let it go and then move forward. Not only move forward figuratively, but literally imagine the future. The commitments kept, the choices made, the desired outcomes, and the trust rebuilt. What does it look like? What does it sound like and what does it feel like? And in the present tense, in the imagined future.

In NLP this is called Future pacing. Imagining the successful future seeing, hearing, and feeling that successful experience as if you are already there.

Our unconscious mind cannot distinguish between a real or imagined thought. It is critical that we imagine a successful future. It has been discovered scientifically that our unconscious mind makes choices before our conscious mind is aware of it. When we clearly command our subconscious mind through future pacing and we see the pathway; and achieving it, how it feels to be there, hearing that success, our subconscious mind believes it and sets out to make the choices, acts upon it and moves us toward it.

The un-restlessness of where we are in the present and the declared where we want to be in the future instead is a powerful motivational tool using cognitive dissonance. From Wikipedia (Cognitive dissonance, 2019) in the field of psychology, cognitive dissonance is the mental discomfort, psychological stress experienced by a person who simultaneously holds two or more contradictory beliefs, ideas, or values.

Always leave the relationship with a vision of the successful future. What does it look like, sound like, and feel like?

Here's an example from my own life about building rapport. I'm going to give you two quick family stories. So, I'm on Facebook as well as all four of my children. I'm not sure that I would be on Facebook near as much if not for my kids. It is the world they have grown up in. It is where they hang out throughout the day. How do you build rapport? People who are like each other, like each other.

My daughter posts a picture of her teenage cat sleeping on social media and it was an opportunity for me to connect with her. I quickly Google cat sleeping funny video and I watch one that has me busting at the seams laughing. I copy and paste the link as a comment to her post. It took me just a few minutes to connect with her, it got a positive reaction from her and it started a conversation.

I do this as much as possible with all my kids. It only takes a few minutes but it lets them know I'm thinking about them, paying attention, and listening to them. It lets then know that I care about them and I want them to smile and laugh. And it maintains rapport.

Can rapport be established by texts, emails, and social media? Yes! It can. It is definitely more challenging than the other forms of communication, like auditory or visual. However, it is possible. Simple and easy.

My second story is more about relationships in breakdown. It is about my son when he was little. We had an argument and he was not happy with me about it. He was sitting on the floor playing a video game, ignoring me. I wanted to talk more about the problem from earlier that day and yet we were not in rapport. So, I plopped myself down next to him and decided to get in rapport with him so we could have a talk.

I didn't have a game controller so I pretended to have one and was playing and moving with my hands, matching his movements, gestures, and expressions. This got his attention pretty quickly and he stopped playing and looked at me. I also stopped and ignored his gaze at me thus matching his behavior of ignoring me.

When he went back to playing, I then continued. He said "What are you doing" I stopped and said "Nothing." and smiled. Now this is where I began to lead and pace our rapport. Me leading him and him matching me. This is at an unconscious level to the other person usually. He smiled back at me. I laughed. He laughed. We were in rapport.

Note you cannot lead and pace until a rapport is established. And also note that rapport was built mostly by saying nothing and just matching his body language. Again, it must be done with integrity to build rapport. It has to be in the context of what would be appropriate within that relationship. Once we established rapport, he was now open to allowing me to speak into his listening and continue a conversation about a challenging subject and confrontation.

One of the last things I want to leave you with is, remember to breathe. It is important that we intentionally take the time every day, several times a day, to breathe deeply and slowly. Breathe on purpose deeply and slowly to calm yourself, to nourish your body and your mind.

Proper breathing is expansive until your belly pushes out. This creates a downward pressure against your vagus nerve that releases the body's natural feel good chemistry, in your body and your mind.

Breathing exercises have these benefits. It calms down the nerves, creates better oxygen supply, lowers your blood pressure, relaxes the muscles, strengthens the lungs and heart, and helps regulate healthy neurology.

When life gets overwhelming take a deep breath in and release it twice as slowly. Be Healthy, Be Well and Be Excellent with building rapport, clarity in your communication, keeping your commitments, and building authentic trust with your relationships, for your family, friends, and with those you love.

**Releasing Negative Emotion**

**– 10 Things**

1. Take a deep breath and let it out twice as slow. Think of a time when you felt that negative emotion. Where is that feeling in your body? Physically move that feeling from where it use to be, and move it to the outside of your body. Place it somewhere that feels good. Does that feeling have a color? Change the color. Change its attributes to how you want it to feel instead. Light or dim. Pulsing or constant. One color or multi-colored. Change it to how you want to feel instead. Notice the direction of that feeling. Grab that feeling and spin it in the opposite direction. Move it faster and faster and faster. Now double how fast you spin it and double it again. Notice how it feels different. Take a deep breath in and let it out twice as slow. Pull that new feeling back into your body. Think of that event and think of the way it used to feel and notice how does it feel different instead. Go into the future, imagine a time where a similar event or person that would have triggered that old feeling and notice how you feel instead now.

2. Exercise – go to the chapter on health and learn more about everything on health. Move your body! Take a walk around the block. Go walk your dog. Turn on the radio and dance. Moving your body releases stress and brings in feeling good and peace in your life.

3. Meditation or simply breathing deeply. Take in a deep breath and exhale out that energy twice as slowly. Take another deep breath in and breathe out twice as slowly. If the emotion is strong, focus on your

breathing. That is all you need in any moment. Let the breathing nourish your body. Let the breath heal your mind. With every breath nourishment flows in and exhale out twice as slow, exhale that energy.

4. Distract yourself in a healthy way. Start something new. Learn something new. Get your mind busy. If a negative feeling permeates the activity, talk to that emotion as if it is a child and it will not get its way.

5. Imagine the opposite emotional state – we cannot hold onto two thoughts at the same time. Play full out for fun! If you feel sad go back to a time when you felt ridiculous JOY! See that joy through your own eyes, how does it feel? If you are feeling anxious and anticipating something negative happening, play this out as full out positive surprise. Go back to a time when you were the most surprised in a positive way in your life. Practice anything that is in a positive direction and notice how your state changes. Practice gratitude, love and kindness. When you send this out into the world it returns back to you.

Gratitude – Anger

Excitement - Fear

Humility – Arrogance

Patience - Frustration

Love – Hate

Surprise - Panic

Sympathy – Cruelty

Charity – Jealousy

Joy – Grief

Interest - Boredom

6. Watch comedy. Fire your funny mirror neurons and feel fabulous. Watching comedy and hearing others laugh will get you out of your funk! Just like when someone yawns and you can't help but yawn, experiencing humor will create the same feeling and laughing in your body. You can't laugh and not feel good at the same time. Even acting laughing will generate feeling good in your body and your mind. Practice with me now. Hahahahaha hahahahaha hahahahaha hohoho hohohohoho haha hahahahahaha – are you smiling now? That's right!

7. Talk with a trusted friend. Schedule a weekly coffee meet up and just talk about anything or nothing at all.

8. Journaling. Express the emotion. Just getting it out on paper feels good. As well as in the future, going back and seeing how you use to feel and how much you have grown and progressed.

9. Smile – You can't smile and not feel good. It actually takes more muscles to frown than it does to smile. Takes some practice but build those physical smile muscles and feel that happiness within you. Share your smile with a stranger and it becomes contagious.

10. Self-care. Get a massage, get a pedicure, get a haircut, read a book. How do you know when you are responsibly taking care of yourself and how does it feel? Do that! You are worth it.

**We all deserve to be happy ( :**

This is something I remind myself of again and again and again. If you are not happy when someone else is happy, it is ok to feel that way and it is also ok that they feel that way. Sometimes just saying we all deserve to be happy is worth saying even when we do not feel happy.

Wish others well. Because if you send out that energy that you do not want others happy, it will return to you.

AND it is ok for you to be happy. You should not feel guilty for feeling happy, being successful, doing great things. AND it is ok if others do not feel that way. Wish others well and when you set that clear intention out into the world, it will return to you.

**Difficult Conversations**

All feelings are valid. When working on conflict resolution sometimes it can be valuable to somewhat disassociate emotionally and look at conflict logically. Imagine there is a movie playing. The actors, you and someone else in the drama are on the movie screen. You are an observer in the front row of a theater watching the movie and the problem. You can see, hear and feel both points of view and you can see the big picture also, a view that each individual cannot see. You have a remote control that you can pause, rewind, fast forward and share with the other person in the conflict.

Roll the movie. Allow it flow timeless and simultaneous. You have a heightened sense of empathy, understanding and knowing. Everything you thought you knew and everything you know now. Jump into the movie as yourself. See what you saw, feel what you felt and hear what you heard. Play the movie of the problem start to finish. Start the movie at a safe place just a moment before the problem happened. Play from start to finish and let it roll just a few moments after the problem to a safe point to stop after the problem occurred. What do you notice? What is important to you about this problem? What is it that you want? What do you fear? What commitments were made, kept or broken by you or them? What is the other person in the conflict not seeing, hearing or feeling? What do you want to say to them?

_____

_____

_____

_____

_____

Jump out of the movie and back into your seat. Do you smell popcorn? I like Twizzlers myself. Okay, jump back into the movie as the other person. You are now that person. See what they see, feel what they feel and hear what they hear. Play the movie of the problem start to finish. Start the movie at a safe place just a moment before the problem happened. Play from start to finish and let it roll just a few moments after the problem to a safe point to stop after the problem occurred. What do you notice different from their perspective? What is important to you about this problem? What is it that you want? What do you fear? What commitments were made, kept or broken by you or them? What is the other person in the conflict not seeing, hearing or feeling? What do you want to say to them?

_____

_____

_____

# DIVORCE PARTY

_____

_____

_____

_____

Jump out of the movie and back into your seat. Do you smell popcorn? I think someone burned the popcorn. Please stop talking during the movie. I don't want to miss the best part! Now let's watch the movie one more time. Play the movie of the problem start to finish. What do you notice that both people do not see? What is important about this problem? What is it that they want? What do they fear? What commitments were made, kept or broken by them? What is the other person in the conflict not seeing, hearing or feeling? What do you want to say to them?

_____

_____

_____

_____

_____

_____

_____

_____

## Confrontation Styles

We possibly have a favorite go to move or style when it comes to conflict. Often, we only see, hear, and feel the problem through our own perspective and through our own eyes. Another person has an entirely different unique map of the world and meanings they make up about experiences negative and positive. Not seeing the other persons perspective, might just be the problem. Understanding, empathy and seeing another's point of view can help to avoid escalating the conflict and work toward recommitting to rebuilding the relationship and building trust in a relationship. And just like exercise the more you practice the better you get with it. The five main ways we deal with confrontation.

*Avoiding* – does not address issue and does nothing to solve the problem. Removing oneself from the problem, letting others deal with it.

*Smoothing* – acting as if everything is fine even though just underneath the surface there could be significant conflict building pressure, agreeing to disagree but not resolving anything.

*Forcing* – Pushing aggressively your needs and not considering the other person's needs. This is considered a win – lose.

*Bargaining* – compromising. This can have positive benefits short term but does nothing to resolve underlying issues.

*Conflict Resolution* – intentionally working toward a resolution where the underlying issue is surfaced and addressed. A recommitment to the relationship is made. This is a win win. This method takes more effort, commitment and over time like exercise, honing the skill of conflict resolution will allow the relationship to grow stronger and build trust with positive outcomes for all parties.

### * * * Conflict Resolution * * *

*The structure for THIS isn't Fuc%ing working.*

*It is a good idea to create some ground rules and agreements when we are going into a conflict resolution. Some possibility examples:*

A. Be nice, be respectful, be clear and agree on what this means.

B. Don't assume, ask for clarity.

C. Look for common ground.

D. Be accountable, own your choices and account for your choices made.

E. Hold others accountable to what they committed to. Call them out on broken commitments.

F. Be willing to see someone else's point of view

G. Say what you mean and mean what you say.

H. Be open to anything, there are no stupid questions.

I. Take turns addressing issues.

J. Not interrupting while the person who's turn it is to talk is talking unless asked permission.

K. Start with the goal in mind first, what would everyone consider a win? Then work backwards.

L. Agreeing to keep voices and tones low, slow and appropriate.

M. No personal language attacks.

N. Setting the intention to resolve a challenge or turn it into an opportunity.

O. Speaking with the "I feel" language and avoid saying things like "you".

P. Instead of asking why ask how … ? "How … ?" has a softer inquiring intention underneath. "Why … ? is more judging and accusatory.

Q. Make requests, do not demands do not give ultimatums.

R. Let's begin!

1. WE NEED TO TALK. There is an elephant in the room! Do not ignore, avoid, or dance around the jiggling pressure cooker waiting for it to blow. Make this easy and take the initiative to say "Hey we have a problem." Get clarity that there is a break down in the relationship and say what it is.

_____

_____

_____

_____

_____

_____

2. WHAT IS THE PROBLEM? Going back to the three elements of every relationship; communication, commitments, and trust at least one of these three elements is not working. What is the commitment that has been compromised? If it is about trust then what is the commitment or agreement that was broken?

_____

_____

_____

_____

_____

_____

3. ARE WE COMMITTED TO RESOLVE THIS? Now is the time for all parties to be clear on what they are committed to for resolution of the problem.

- I am committed to be clear with my communication and what is expected.

- I am committed to doing what I say.

- I will keep my commitments because

I value trust in this relationship.

_____

_____

_____

4. MAKE A PLAN.

What are the requests I will make?

What, who, by when?

What resources will I need?

What actions will I take?

5. TAKE ACTION. Do what you say you are committed to.

Pick a relationship that you want to work on; self, family, friend, or work and fill out a relationship S.M.A.R.T. Goal below.

**Relationship S.M.A.R.T. Goal (Meyer, 2019)**

**What is the Goal?** (Written in the future tense as if already achieved)

_____

_____

_____

**S - Specific.**

What will the goal accomplish?

_____

_____

_____

How and why will it be accomplished?

_____

_____

_____

**M - Measurable.**

How will you measure whether or not the goal has been reached (list at least two indicators)?

_____

_____

_____

**A - Achievable.**

Is it possible?

_____
_____
_____

Have others done it successfully?

_____
_____
_____

Do you have the necessary knowledge, skills, abilities, and resources to accomplish the goal?

_____
_____
_____

Will meeting the goal challenge you without defeating you?

_____
_____
_____

**R - Results-focused.**

What is the reason, purpose, or benefit of accomplishing the goal?

_____
_____
_____

What is the outcome result (not the activities leading up to the result) of the goal?

_____
_____
_____

**T - Time-based.**

What is the established completion date and does that completion date create a practical sense of urgency?

_____
_____
_____

Revised Goal:

_____
_____
_____
_____
_____
_____

Notes:

_____
_____
_____

# DIVORCE PARTY

# Chapter 6
## Finances 1-2-3

"Too many people spend money they haven't earned, to buy things they don't want, to impress people they don't like." Will Smith

"You can have everything in life you want, if you will just help other people get what they want." Zig Ziglar

### What you will get in this chapter

- ✓ How to be financially fit and fabulous!
- ✓ Peace - the value of getting finances in order
- ✓ The only stupid question is the one you don't ask
- ✓ Quit bouncing checks is money in the bank
- ✓ Get peace by taking care of these 4 things
- ✓ Pay with cash and you will spend less – human nature
- ✓ Murphy's law and why you need a rainy-day fund
- ✓ Get out of debt – reducing then annihilating
- ✓ Quick and easy budget to get control of it - all FAST
- ✓ Pay off your home QUICK - I did it in 6 years
- ✓ How giving to charity or a cause increases happiness

### How to be financially- $$$ fit and fabulous!

Finances were my biggest challenge going through my divorce. I made decent money for a blue-color worker as a licensed passenger elevator/escalator mechanic. But I had no structure, habit's, or support to lean into. I had a belief that it was something I was not good at and could never figure out. It was just who I was. I would always be in financial chaos and drowning in debt.

I had been listening to motivational books and had heard some of the principles with self-development including N.L.P. The N.L.P. Neuro linguistic programming model is the study of excellence. You have heard this before, if someone else can do it, so can you.

Proximity is key. By proximity meaning getting as close as possible to the person to observe the person. Even if the person is no longer alive, you can get close to them by means of reading biographies, documents, historical accounts, journals, watching documentaries or movies, listening to audio recordings, albums, cassettes, or digital media. Success leaves clues. And our mirror neurons mirror, and will take that success, try it on and integrate it into our body, mind, and spirit. Consciously and subconsciously. If you want to be broke get close to broke people with their mind set and habits. If you want to be financially fit, hang out with those people who have those habits and behaviors.

How to be financially fit and fabulous is easy, just like searching on Google, the answers are all already there. We have all the answers already! BUT we don't always ask the right question. You may be starting from scratch or maybe you need help with budgeting or investing. Knowing the right question IS the right answer. Without the right question, you are cast into darkness. Now more than ever in the history of the planet there are more resources than there ever was, right at your fingertips if you have the right question. The right question is the answer. The right question gets you to close proximity of success and the trail to it. What is your monthly income are your expenses?

Knowledge is power! This is just a start and beginning place to get your feet wet in budgeting. Often when you list your income the question arises, "Where does all that money go?"

1) Write down your total <u>monthly</u> income after taxes from all sources. If you get paid bi-weekly, multiply by 26 (26 bi-weekly months in a year) and divide by 12 (months) to get monthly income. If you get paid weekly, multiply by 52 and divide by twelve to get monthly income.

2) List your expenses as <u>monthly</u>. You have regular bills occurring monthly, but also try to consider all other bills that are not regular like quarterly and yearly expenses. Also list all the other expenses like gas, food, subscriptions, clothes, entertainment, and birthdays. You must account down to the dollar everything that you know you purchase. For a yearly bill divide by 12 to get the monthly amount. For a bi-weekly bill multiply by 26 (26 bi weeks in a year) and divide by 12 (months) to get the monthly amount. For a bi-yearly bill multiply times 2 and divide by 12. For a quarterly bill, multiply times 4 and then divide by twelve to get monthly amount.

3) Subtract the expense total from the income. Dave calls this zero-based budgeting. This will let you know that every dollar has a place. Ensure that you are not over or under but exactly zero-balanced.

**Notes:**

_____

_____

_____

_____

_____

_____

## DIVORCE PARTY

| | Starting Point Budget | | |
|---|---|---|---|
| **1.** Income 1 | | | |
| Income 2 | | | |
| Income 3 | | | |
| | | | |
| **2. Expenses** | | | |
| | | | |
| **Savings** | | **Clothing** | |
| Emergency Fund | | Adults | |
| Birthdays | | Kids | |
| Holidays | | | |
| TOTAL | | TOTAL | |
| | | | |
| **House** | | **Other** | |
| Rent | | Heath Insurance | |
| Mortgage | | Life Insurance | |
| Maintenance / Repair | | Entertainment | |
| Real Estate Tax | | Baby Sitter | |
| TOTAL | | TOTAL | |
| **Food** | | **Utilities** | |
| Family | | Power | |
| Pets | | Water | |
| TOTAL | | Phone | |
| | | Waste | |
| | | Cable | |
| | | Internet | |
| **Vehicle** | | Cell | |
| Car loan 1 | | TOTAL | |
| Car Loan 2 | | | |
| Tires | | **Savings** | |
| Gas | | **House** | |
| Oil Change | | **Food** | |
| Repairs | | **Vehicle** | |
| TOTAL | | **Clothing** | |
| | | **Other** | |
| | | **Utilities** | |
| | | **Total Expenses** | |
| | | | |
| | | Total Income | |
| | | (minus) Total Expenses | |
| | | **Zero-Balance?** | |

## Peace - the value of getting- Your finances in order

There was a time when I was going through my divorce that I was living literally in the darkness, the power was shut off and the house was being foreclosed on. I was never good with my finances and paying bills. I had piles of unopened bills with no idea when they were due. I knew my bills were due when things would get shut off and sadly, sometimes I had the money in my account, but then would get zapped with disconnect fees, reconnect fees, NSF charges and bleeding to death in my own ignorance. I had both a financial crisis and organization problem.

I was on my way to literally becoming homeless and not even having a place to call my home. I would have to visit my kids, well I don't know where, maybe the park. Being homeless didn't concern me as much as the shame I felt, where I was at this point in my life. I felt hopeless. How did I let this all happen? What kind of father was I, to be where I was at in life?

In the middle of my divorce crisis, I knew I needed financial help and guidance, fast. I had been listening to a financial radio program on and off for a couple years and there had always been a calling to me, this was something I needed to do. The endless stories, callers, and testimonials from students of his, who had their lives go from train wreck to transformation and Financial Freedom were powerful, believable, and endless.

Often, I would feel better about my own situation, hearing the ridiculous choices people were making and how deep in the hole they were compared to me. Righteously, I would pat myself on the back, "my hole isn't that deep!"

He had a program that anyone could attend. It was a Christian-based program but it was not a heavy beat you over the head with the bible approach. Just occasional quotes from the bible, how it applied to finance and choices. Basically scripturally-backed advice. I am Christian and I really was attracted to this guy and interested in his program.

David Ramsey's Financial Peace University, (Financial Peace University, 2019) F.P.U. I looked online and found a class that was starting in about 4 weeks. There was a minimal investment of about $100 at the time. I was hesitant to trust that the value was worth the $100. I was a little skeptical to spend that kind of money considering the situation I was in and how far that $100 would otherwise go for gas or food.

My gut told me or perhaps the spirit within me pushed me to knowing – you have to do this, you have to get this part of your life in order, to be a good father, clean this mess up NOW! And I still had to wait for about a month for the class to start, and that wait is what I hung all of my last hopes on.

"And a servant who knows what the master wants, but is not prepared and doesn't carry out those instructions, will be severely punished. But someone who does not know, and then does something wrong, will be punished only lightly. When someone has been given much, much will be required in return; and when someone has been entrusted with much, even more will be required." Luke 12:47-48

I showed up in the parking lot and my negative self-talk was kicking in. I thought what good could this class do? This is a waste of time and now, a waste of money already spent. I really don't feel like being social right now. How am I ever going to survive this mess I am in? God, I am such an idiot. I was ready to turn around and leave several times. I remember getting lost while walking through the church trying to find the meeting room, and THAT was another almost excuse to leave. I finally persisted beyond my internal dialog, and decided to stay. But it was really, really, really close to not happening many times.

I was welcomed in and immediately felt I was in the right place. I had been waiting for almost 30 days to be here. Despite all my internal negative talk, limiting beliefs, and multiple close-calls of just quitting, I was now with others who were not judging me but being compassionate. I had felt hopeless and despair. Now was the beginning of hope, and hope is something that I hadn't seen for a long time.

All are welcome in the program. No matter what your religion or beliefs, all are welcome. Although the FPU is based on David Ramsey and his experience from his financial ruin and bankruptcy to financial freedom and abundance, it is palatable for even the non-church goer. No singing of kum-by-ya or awkward rituals, etc. Pretty straight forward and to the point, the meeting lasting about an hour. The Meeting format is: group welcome/opening, video, end discussion and homework assignment, then dismissal till the next week's meeting.

The class is structured in such a way to give you hope that is a relief and action steps to move you forward and toward the right direction of financial peace and good choices. That very first night I left with an incredible new hope that I didn't have or feel before the class started. It was a stress relief for me and felt incredible hope that things were absolutely going to get better.

The take away from the first class was that I needed to create a safe place for me and my finances. A safe place from bill collectors, creditors, and toxic people, that were counterproductive to my spiritual and financial healing.

*The only stupid question is the one you don't ask!*

Beware of the negative self-talk that will appear. Pride is, after all, one of the 7 deadly sins. And if you are a man, a big part of who we are is being the provider. If you are a woman, it is more about having security. If you have any questions, now is the time to play full out and let go of the ego. The ego actually caused this mess. The only way to wisdom is asking the right questions. Surrounding yourself with people who have a nurturing way about them, love, and support you exactly how you are. You will find this growth environment in the David Ramsey program.

**Quit bouncing checks- is money in the bank?**

I don't want to spend much time on the obvious, but when finances are in a mess, not organized and managed, not knowing where the money is and isn't, when bills are happening and not happening, bouncing checks is almost guaranteed. Knowing what all your expenses are and writing them down with the dates they are due is an excellent first step.

We have to be able to take a snapshot of the truth of money coming in and going out. Learning how to budget is coming up in this chapter. Master it. Master knowing what comes in and manage what goes out. NSF fees, utility hook-up fees, ATM use charges are simply lazy wasteful money management. No judgment from me. That is exactly where I was. Master your money or it will always slip through your fingers.

### Sleep well by taking- care of these 4 things

Dave talks about the 4 pillars of finance that creates a safe space between you and the world. You have to take care of what is most important first and this will create a secure place that you can rest, sleep and recharge your life as you reorganize your life.

You must take care of these 4 things first. Pay these first before anything else, otherwise your efforts will get sabotaged and without these four things, chaos with your financial security ensues. The 4 things are: housing, utilities, food, and transportation. It can be challenging when a rude, obnoxious bill collector wants to strong arm us into commitments that may devastate our safe space and compromise the 4 walls.

Getting clarity on the bills that must come first will help you to say no to rude, obnoxious creditors. They often want to talk you into an agreement that is not in your best interest but only in their best interest. I am not saying don't pay your debts. I am saying that you have to take care of these 4 financial walls first so that you can breathe a little. This lets you protect your needs, and your families so that you can think, sleep and find peace in your home in the middle of the storm. The 4 walls will ground you so that you can work on getting out of debt and moving forward on the road to financial freedom and abundance.

### Pay with cash and you will- spend less – human nature

Dave introduces a powerful financial system, using envelopes that help you get control of your money immediately! You budget out your expenses, and key expenses like gas, food, entertainment, etc. is all accounted for. The beautiful thing about the envelope system is that it freezes your money and you have it in your hands. If you are immediately challenged with balancing your checkbook, the envelope system will help alleviate several problems. If an automatic payment comes out, zapping your checking account, while dealing with that avalanche mess, you still have cash for the necessities (the 4 walls).

For now, anyway, you can still breathe knowing you have a home, vehicle, utilities, and food. The biggest attraction of the envelope system is that it is a fact we spend less. It has been proven scientifically that we spend less money when we physically have to hand out cash. There is a real neurological pain that is experienced when spending cash that is not felt when using credit cards. There is even less association with pain when you wave instead of swipe a credit/debit card and farther association with pain when using smart phone apps and smart watch pay.

Understanding the envelope system, and honoring the 4 financial walls of financial safety, deactivates the fight/flight response. Meaning you can sleep at night. It gives you confidence and power over your money by letting you make choices that best serve you and not the bill collectors.

I remember the drive home from that first Financial Peace University class and being so excited for a brighter future to come. I also began to hear my internal dialog again, fears and self-doubt. Would how I felt and the vision of the brighter future I felt in class make it all the way home with me and continue the next day?

### Step 1 - Murphy's law and why you need a rainy-day fund

In David Ramsey's FPU he introduces his 7 baby steps. We will not go over all the steps for the purposes of this chapter. Assuming you are here and in a financial mess or "challenge" or opportunity? We want to get effective fast and stop the bleeding out of cash. Kind of like triaging, however with finances we triage depending upon where you are at in a set of sequential steps. We start at the beginning first step with the most important financial baby step that starts to protect you financially from Murphy's law and rainy days. Then onward to more important baby steps that further protect your financial health. It is recommended the steps are in order and you finish the first before the second before the third and so on. The plan is to protect you fast and then work toward savings and getting out of debt.

David suggests first with saving for a rainy day. He calls it the emergency fund and suggests saving $1000. Get $1000 saved as quickly as possible for an emergency. Emergencies are not unplanned. You can count on them to happen, and they absolutely will, guaranteed. The $1000 is a buffer to not spiral your 4 walls out of control and plunge you even deeper into debt. The game is to become financially free and first we want to start with financial stability.

There are all kinds of ways to get the cash saved including, selling everything you don't need, have a rummage sale, work part-time. The interesting thing is that when you have the emergency fund, it acts like Murphy's law repellent. This seems to be the way the universe works. Abundance attracts abundance.

### Step 2 - Get out of debt reducing then annihilating

The next baby step is the debt snowball. There are many ways to reduce debt but David suggests this method that gives you the quickest feedback of success. Then your brain drops dopamine and that feels good. A great way to build a strong habit long term.

1. Make a list of all your debts and amounts.

2. List them in the order of lowest to highest.

3. After completing your budget (later in the chapter), and after accounting for the expenses that make up home, car, utilities, and food, as well as all other needed expenses, now you can start to pay your debt down. Make minimum payments on the largest amount debts, and a maximum payment toward the smallest debt with the understanding what you can account for and afford in your budget and what is left over to pay your debts.

4. Once the lowest debt is paid off, CELEBRATE. Then move to the next lowest debt. Pay what you had been paying on the first debt (now paid off), toward the second debt. As you pay off the debt, it begins to snowball and your debt payments will increase and overcome your debt until you are debt free!

| Creditor | Total Debt | Min Payment | Min + Extra Payment | New Payment |
|---|---|---|---|---|
| Coffee Club Card | $125 | $25 | 25+50 | $75 |
| Shoes R Us | $250 | $45 | 45+75 | $120 |
| Very Best Buy | $625 | $95 | 95+120 | $215 |
| Visa Card | $937 | $10 | 10+215 | $225 |
| Car Loan | $12,000 | $337 | 337+225 | $562 |
| Motorcycle | $17,000 | $378 | 378+562 | $940 |
| Boat | $23,000 | $425 | 225+940 | $1165 |

Notes:

_____

_____

_____

_____

| Creditor | Total Debt | Min Payment | Min + Extra Payment | New Payment |
|---|---|---|---|---|
|  |  |  |  |  |
|  |  |  |  |  |
|  |  |  |  |  |
|  |  |  |  |  |
|  |  |  |  |  |
|  |  |  |  |  |
|  |  |  |  |  |
|  |  |  |  |  |
|  |  |  |  |  |
|  |  |  |  |  |

## Step 3 - Fully Funded- Emergency Fund

FPU's baby step 3 is a fully funded emergency fund. This includes having your $1000 emergency fund and 3-6 month's expenses in a savings account that you do not touch. This is a long-term goal and you are not there yet. But imagine the security and how you would feel knowing that if you lost your job, you can maintain your 4 walls of security for 3-6 months. What peace that would bring for you and those in your life.

I get paid absolutely nothing to say this, but I highly encourage you to look at the David Ramsey Financial Peace University Program. It is life changing. I have gone through the program 7 times and twice with 2 of my 4 children. It costs about $129 at the writing of this book and that is about $14.33 per class of the 9-week program. You can find out more information free online, YouTube, and you will find people singing their praise of how it has absolutely changed their financial life around. Dave Ramsey FPU Financial Peace University

There were so many personal ah-has in the FPU course. When I did my first budget, I didn't understand how I had so much left over on paper after my monthly bills were subtracted from my income. Digging a little deeper, and looking at the quarterly and yearly expenses, you start to realize where all the money goes over the year. There are birthdays, licenses, dues, and drama that pops up throughout the year, a flat tire, bearings go out on your car, etc.

There are 7 total baby steps and I did not want to overwhelm you without the loving support you will find in a David Ramsey class. Some of the steps may even seem laughable as to how could that even be possible. I am here to tell you that it is absolutely possible and quicker than you can imagine if you get started right now!

"The best time to plant a tree was 20 years ago. The second-best time is now." - *Chinese Proverb*

**David Ramsey - Baby Steps**

From his Book – The Financial Peace Planner (Ramsey D. L., 1998)

**BABY STEP 1**

Save $1,000 for your starter emergency fund.

**BABY STEP 2**

Pay off all debt (except the house) using the debt snowball.

**BABY STEP 3**

Save 3–6 months of expenses in a fully-funded emergency fund.

**BABY STEP 4**

Invest 15% of your household income in retirement.

**BABY STEP 5**

Save for your children's college fund.

**BABY STEP 6**

Pay off your home early.

**BABY STEP 7**

Build wealth and give.

The budgeting knowledge that I learned in FPU was invaluable and the program covers everything with your finances and more including: insurance, being frugal, how to make deals, creditors, saving money, borrowing money, legal documents like having a last Will and Testament. I have taken the FPU class in person, presently 6 times, and purchased the DVD's that are used in the class. I watch the DVD's at least once a year to remind me of what I have learned and more importantly, re-ignite my fire to be excellent with my finances.

### Quick and easy budget- to get control of it all FAST

Having said all that about the FPU program, I want to share a personal system that is quick and dirty and has worked excellent for me. I still use it to this day. To be honest, I hate balancing my check book. Keep in mind there were times during the divorce, that even brushing my teeth felt like the hardest thing in the world for me, I had to force myself to do it. I kind of did a mash-up of FPU's budget system.

**This is for you if:**

- You don't know how to balance your checkbook
- You are late paying bills, accumulating late fees on top of that
- Auto payments are causing a catastrophe to checking account
- You are overwhelmed and feel out of control with your bills and paying them

This takes a little time initially but it's so worth it! Once you do it you will feel relieved and more in control, knowing your expenses are organized, by date and amount and how they need to be paid. At any given moment, you will be able to take a glance at this list and know what's happening in your check book and what's coming up, avoid making bad financial choices that snowball, NSF fees, late fees, etc.

Here's what you do:

1. Make a list of expenses; monthly, yearly, bi-yearly, quarterly, weekly, biweekly, etc. that involves your checking, credit, an important bill that must be paid or is on automatic deduct or charge.

2. Sequentially place bills in the order due in the month.

3. Include the amounts for each expense.

4. Include payment method: automatic, check, online.

5. Make a list of any checks you have written and sticky note them to the form below, until they clear.

After you gather all the information above and fill out the form on the following page you will have some clarity and some important information organized so that you can make financial decisions today.

1. You will know what bills are automatic and when they will happen so that you insure there is money in the account to cover it.

2. You know what bills are happening today and what bills happen every day. You know when to pay your bills.

3. If you have to mail a check you will know the lead time to get it there on time.

4. This will show you how well dispersed your bills are versus when you get paid. Possibly rearranging bill due dates in sync with your check is beneficial to not strain 1 week over another.

This will require you to gather all the information, find old bills or open your banking online and retrieve all the known expenses. It is also a big time saver to make a cheat sheet list of financial user names and passwords. Not having the information at your fingertips when you need them can create analysis paralysis and procrastination. Make it safe and super quick to access when you need the information by coding your cheat sheet or storing in a locked safe. You can code the username and or passwords by leaving out the first or last character or symbol to prevent someone logging in if your list was found.

Make this easy and do it in easy chunked down steps. Start just listing all the expenses on a piece of paper. Next, one -by-one, find that bill in paper or online, and write down on your list next to that bill, the due date and amount. Some bills like property tax or car license or insurance may be a little more challenging to find because of their infrequencies. Again, just know that your upfront effort is going to be well worth it! This creates clarity and foresight of those wildcard bills so they don't sneak up on you and catch you off guard or traumatize your checking account. This will give you confidence and security protecting your four financial walls.

Notes:

_____

_____

_____

_____

_____

_____

_____

_____

_____

_____

# DIVORCE PARTY

## Monthly and Non Monthly Bills

© Copyright David Youhas 2019

Method: C=cash or check * AD=auto payment * AC=debit auto payment checking
Frequency: M=monthly Q=quarterly BY=bi yearly Y=yearly W-weekly

| Week | Due Date | Send Date | Amount | Check # | Description | Frequency | Method |
|---|---|---|---|---|---|---|---|
| 1 | | | | | internet | | M |
| | | | | | gas/electric | | M |
| | | | | | car insurance | | M |
| | | | | | health insurance | | |
| 2 | | | | | mortgage | | M |
| | | | | | phone | | |
| | | | | | credit card 1 | | M |
| 3 | | | | | auto loan | | M |
| | | | | | cell phone | | M |
| | | | | | home insurance | | M |
| 4 | | | | | water/sewer | | M |
| | | | | | credit card 2 | | M |
| | | | | | gym | | Q |
| Non Monthly | | | | | | | |
| | | | | | car 1 license | | Y |
| | | | | | union dues | | Q |
| | | | | | car 2 license | | Y |
| | | | | | property tax | | Y |
| | | | | | tollway EZ Pass | | Y |
| | | | | | birthdays | | Y |
| | | | | | clothes | | Q |
| | | | | | food | | W |
| | | | | | oil change | | Q |
| | | | | | newspaper subscription | | BY |
| | | | | | | | |
| | | | | | | | |
| | | | | | | | |
| | | | | | | | |

# DIVORCE PARTY

**Monthly and Non Monthly Bills** © Copyright David Youhas 2019
Method: C=cash or check * AD=auto payment * AC=debit auto payment checking
Frequency: M=monthly Q=quarterly BY=bi yearly Y=yearly W-weekly

| Week | Due Date | Send Date | Amount | Check # | Description | Frequency | Method |
|---|---|---|---|---|---|---|---|
| 1 | | | | | | | |
| | | | | | | | |
| | | | | | | | |
| | | | | | | | |
| | | | | | | | |
| 2 | | | | | | | |
| | | | | | | | |
| | | | | | | | |
| | | | | | | | |
| 3 | | | | | | | |
| | | | | | | | |
| | | | | | | | |
| | | | | | | | |
| 4 | | | | | | | |
| | | | | | | | |
| | | | | | | | |
| | | | | | | | |
| Non Monthly | | | | | | | |
| | | | | | | | |
| | | | | | | | |
| | | | | | | | |
| | | | | | | | |
| | | | | | | | |
| | | | | | | | |
| | | | | | | | |
| | | | | | | | |
| | | | | | | | |
| | | | | | | | |
| | | | | | | | |
| | | | | | | | |
| | | | | | | | |

This is a big first step to mastering your finances. The good news is that it gets easier and all your work was well worth the effort. Whether you do this on paper or electronically with a spread sheet. The information, numbers, dates, and amounts will be pretty constant. And it is always easy to edit a change and view where you are at any time. Congratulations for finishing this step moving you toward mastering your finances.

**Pay off your home QUICK - I did in 6 years**

Paying off your home or even owning a home might seem too good to be true. Maybe you are renting. In the middle of my divorce I was renting and it felt like I was throwing away money. Now there are actually good reasons to rent a home. There is nothing wrong with renting and it might be the right choice for you. Depending on work and possibly having to move around to new areas of the country, it might be a good reason to rent. You can take advantage of the liquid nature of commitment and get to know a town and what community would interest you without the long-term commitment that buying a home has. Maybe you are considering moving and renting is a good option. There are many good reasons to rent and they all have a purpose why that is the right choice.

I knew that I wanted to be around my children and I knew that it was the right choice for me to move toward financial freedom. I come from a frugal nature and I am a fixer upper kind of guy. Besides, everything you need to learn how to work on a home is online, with the right question!

This might not be for you ... but it was for me! I was often inspired by the stories I heard on David Ramsey's radio show. Hearing the results that people were getting and the extremes that people would go to with what he calls gazelle intensity!

One of the things David says a lot is "sell the car." People are spending more on their car than on their home and flipping their finances upside down. In fact, an upside-down loan is a potentially dangerous trap. Upside-down means you owe more on the debt than the debt is worth. This happens the second you drive a new vehicle off a car lot. Instantly loosing value 9 – 11% and then 20% or more each year.

How quickly a new car depreciates. It begins as soon as 1 minute after you drive it the car off of the car lot. David Ramsey's (Ramsey, 2019) from his article "New Car vs Used Car"

| Initial Vehicle Value | $35,000.00 | Total Lost (Approx.) Value | LOST! |
|---|---|---|---|
| New Car Value After... | | | |
| 1 minute (driving off of car lot) | $31,500.00 | 9-11% | $3,500.00 |
| 1 year (after only 12 months) | $28,000.00 | 20.00% | $7,000.00 |
| 2 years | $24,500.00 | 30.00% | $10,500.00 |
| 3 years | $21,000.00 | 40.00% | $14,000.00 |
| 4 years | $18,500.00 | 50.00% | $16,500.00 |
| 5 years | $15,000.00 | 60.00% | $20,000.00 |

AFTER ONE MINUTE: If you buy a shiny new $35,000 car, it loses somewhere between 9–11% of its value the moment you drive off the lot. You're basically throwing $3,500 out the car window as you drive the car home for the first time!

AFTER ONE YEAR: Fast-forward 12 months and that car sitting in your driveway will have lost around 20% or maybe even more of its value from the day you bought it.

AFTER FIVE YEARS: You can expect your new car to lose 60% of its value after driving it around for five years.(3) Most cars lose about 10% of their value every year after that steep first-year dip.(4)

I was highly motivated with gazelle intensity! I sold the car and even put in the classified advertisement "selling the car because David Ramsey said I had to sell the car" and purchased a used vehicle that made more financial sense. I remember a young man like 21 years old. He lived in a space above a garage until he became debt free.

"Live like no one else, so one day you can live like no one else."

*- David Ramsey*

I went out looking for my David Ramsey home. I found that home for $32,000. I paid this home completely off within 6 years. I proudly refer to this home as my David Ramsey fixer upper.

Property tax can be almost as expensive as rent. And if you are spending just as much on property tax than to rent, is owning a home worth owning a home. My property tax is about $350 a year. Imagine the cost of home living being about as little as $29 a month and what you could do with that extra cash instead? Become a master of your finances and go for your financial freedom with gazelle intensity!

"The rich rule over the poor, and the borrower is slave to the lender." *Proverbs 22:7*

Free Yourself!

"Money is not everything, but it ranks right up there with oxygen."

*- Zig Ziglar*

### How giving to charity or a cause increases happiness

It is not a sin to want to be financially free or abundant. Money is amoral. It is like a brick You could smash a car window with it or you could build a children's hospital with it. It is the intention of the person who holds the brick. Money is the same way. You can do some really good things for yourself, those you love, your family, friends, community and the world. Biblically it is not having money that is a sin, but instead the love of money. There is plenty of scripture on money and how it can be used for good and God's work.

**For the love of money is the root of all evil** - *Timothy 6:10*

I just got back from a Tony Robbins event in Miami Florida - Unleash the Power Within and now I can proudly say "YES! I am a Fire Walker!" Tony works with all kinds of people from around the world. He works with famous and everyday people. High performance people, presidents, singers, TV personalities, actors, Olympians, millionaires and billionaires. He talked about how small a percent of those who are wealthy are also happy.

Contribution is a human need. This is not a new concept. Charity and its value are told in the scriptures of the bible. We have all probably heard the story from the Bible of the widows offering. The story about a woman who gave a few pennies at the church offering. And Jesus and his disciples witnessed this.

### The Widow's Offering

41 Jesus sat down opposite the place where the offerings were put and watched the crowd putting their money into the temple treasury.

Many rich people threw in large amounts. **42** But a poor widow came and put in two very small copper coins, worth only a few cents.

**43** Calling his disciples to him, Jesus said, "Truly, I tell you, this poor widow has put more into the treasury than all the others. **44** They all gave out of their wealth; but she, out of her poverty, put in everything—all she had to live on." - *Mark 12:41-44*

The widow gave all she had for her faith in God. Now that is amazing faith. Who has that courage to leap into that sort of blind trust faith? I don't want to turn off my atheist friends and make this a Sunday school. Again, the bible is simply filled with fascinating lessons on human nature. Have you known someone that gave everything they had out of love and expected nothing in return?

The church has other scripture on giving 10% of your income to the church. I remember sitting in on a bible study class once where there was self-solicited bragging about giving. The woman brought up her concern that she was not sure if she should give before taxes or after taxes. This started a slightly heated discussion with the group as she smugly sat back with a slight grin and watched what she had instigated take on a life of its own with the others. And when the time was just right, she interjected condescendingly "Well, I always give before taxes just to be safe."

Increase your happiness by giving and contributing. I want to encourage you to give to charity not to "Look good in the eyes of others." but to look good in your own eyes. To show yourself that YOU appreciate what you have and are living in abundance. You contribute outward and you control your choices to be and do that. Give and expect or demand nothing in return. You give because you are thankful for all that has been given you. And interestingly enough when you reflect outward that openness to giving you will attract abundance back.

No matter where you are in your journey, I want to encourage you to look for opportunities to contribute and help others. With your time, your positive energy and spirit, sharing a smile, giving a hug, volunteering to help others or charitable causes. Give because you love yourself enough to love others in return. We have everything we need inside of us to be happy. Don't horde that love.

In the movie "Citizen Kane," it starts at the end of his life. Kane utters his last words, "Rosebud" before passing. The one thing that brought him great happiness was either a sled from his youth or that moment in time when he was younger. The relationship he had with his family before his parents, who were living in poverty, signed him away to be adopted and raised by a wealthy man who would educate him.

In the story, no one close to Kane knows the meaning of "Rosebud." In the end, all our memories and possessions, are returned to ashes and turned into smoke, that drifts away and vanishes. We can't take our possessions with us when we leave. All that matters when our life is over is how we lived our life before we passed on.

If you don't know how to contribute, give, and love the world, find someone who is already successful at doing it and get close to them. Remember, proximity is key! Fake it till you make it or imagine that you already know how to give. Give all you can from your heart. Give everything you can freely. When you have the intention to contribute to others and the world, shining your reflection of love outward, you will be loved in return. You will see your love reflection, joy and happiness in the eyes, smiles, and laughter of others. Have faith and know this is the right thing to do; a good thing to do. And you will absolutely feel that love and connection in return.

Before wrapping this chapter up with one more exercise, again I want to encourage you to discover the David Ramsey Financial Peace University. Your life and your children's lives will never be the same! If you are challenged with your finances, you cannot afford to stick your head in the sand. Find a class here:

Dave Ramsey Financial Peace University

**Finances S.M.A.R.T Goal (Meyer, 2019)**

Fill out a Finance S.M.A.R.T. Goal form next.

**What is the Goal?** (Written in the future tense as if already achieved)

_____

_____

_____

**S - Specific.**

What will the goal accomplish?

_____

_____

_____

How and why will it be accomplished?

_____

_____

_____

**M - Measurable.**

How will you measure whether or not the goal has been reached (list at least two indicators)?

_____

_____

_____

**A - Achievable.**

Is it possible?

_____

_____

_____

Have others done it successfully?

_____

_____

_____

Do you have the necessary knowledge, skills, abilities, and resources to accomplish the goal?

_____

_____

_____

Will meeting the goal challenge you without defeating you?

_____

_____

_____

### R - Results-focused.

What is the reason, purpose, or benefit of accomplishing the goal?

_____

_____

_____

What is the outcome result (not the activities leading up to the result) of the goal?

_____

_____

_____

### T - Time-based.

What is the established completion date and does that completion date create a practical sense of urgency?

_____

_____

_____

Revised Goal:

_____

DIVORCE PARTY

Notes:

# Chapter 7
## Personal Growth

"Where there is no vision, the people perish..." James 29:18

"A dead thing can go with the stream, but only a living thing can go against it."

- G.K. Chesterton, The Everlasting Man

"For things to change, you have to change. To make yourself more attractive you have to become more attractive"

"Alice: Would you tell me, please, which way I ought to go from here? The Cheshire Cat: That depends a good deal on where you want to get to. Alice: I don't much care where. The Cheshire Cat: Then it doesn't much matter which way you go." - Lewis Carol, Alice In Wonderland

**What you will get in this chapter**

✓ Know thyself – become who you really are

✓ What is the meaning of life? Find your purpose

✓ A sense of direction

✓ Turbo boost your confidence

✓ Get focused, get results

✓ Persistence builds resilience

✓ The wheel of life

✓ Distracting yourself in a healthy way

✓ Manufacture more motivation

✓ Get to the other side of comfortable

✓ 50 Goals exercise – what all do you want?

✓ Design your future NOW

✓ S.M.A.R.T. Goals

✓ 3 P's – Purpose, Products and Process

✓ WFO Well-formed Outcome

✓ Learning moving forward

✓ Edward Deming - The Kaizen Principle

and Continued Self-development

### Know thyself– become who you really are

**The Oracle at Delphi.** The Ancient Greek aphorism "know thyself," is one of the Delphic maxims and was inscribed in the pronaos of the Temple of Apollo at Delphi according to the Greek writer Pausanias. It has inspired countless philosophers, most famously Socrates.

The path to happiness is within us and we can access it at any moment. Go back to a time when you were the happiest in your life. What do you see? What do you hear? How do you feel? Where were you and who were you with? Notice how you feel now. Happiness is a state of mind as is any feeling.

Not pursuing personal growth is like hiding money under a mattress. Hidden and stagnant, money not moving will decrease in value. Not invested means not earning interest, not growing in value. And, as the cost of living and inflation will certainly continue to increase, that stored exchange of work energy, converted into stored energy in the form of money, devalues and decreases.

If we do not invest in self-improvement, we stay exactly the same, the world continues to change and grow. Kindergarteners will eventually pass us by with what they have learned in school, as technology continues to grow. Our skills, capabilities, connections, and resources are becoming obsolete if we do not continually develop. Whole industries and workers have found themselves unemployed overnight. They are now in a world where they are considered undereducated, and who believed their training would keep them safe and employed until retirement.

### What is the meaning of life? Find your purpose

The meaning of life is what we make of it. Everyone has a different meaning and value. The important meaning to life is having a purpose in life. In Viktor Frankl's book "Man's Search For Meaning," he discusses the importance of having a purpose. Viktor Frankl, a survivor of the holocaust, was imprisoned in various camps including Auschwitz. In his book he discusses that those prisoners who had a purpose lived, and the moment a purpose was lost, death would follow.

Not to be grim, but a powerful lesson learned in extreme, unthinkable conditions about human nature and the importance of having a purpose in life. This could easily be overlooked if not intentionally considered. This may be the first time you have ever considered it.

### What is your purpose in life?

To get your brain juices flowing, what do you value in life?

_____

_____

What is the meaning of life to you?

_____

_____

What is your purpose in life?

_____

_____

### Get your sense of direction

Purpose is important, and having a goal to go after is like a flight plan for an airplane. It becomes evident if you are headed in the right direction or in the wrong direction. Have you ever felt like you are aimlessly wondering in life? This is because of not having a sense of direction, a feeling like floating nowhere and everywhere. Having a place to focus on will give your purpose in life a certainty and foundation that you are moving in the right direction toward your aspirations.

### Turbo boost your confidence

When you make a commitment to yourself and others and you keep that commitment, you build trust with others and trust within yourself. This trust co-exists with integrity; you do what you say you are going to do. After you set out to learn a new skill and accomplish it, this builds confidence because now you have evidence that you can do it.

If you do not have confidence it is that you have possibly broken your word with others and also yourself. Trust can be rebuilt and so can confidence. Build your confidence with willingness to reach outside of your comfort zone. Build new skills and keep learning and growing.

### Get focused, get results.

Practice focusing builds resilience to focus like a muscle. As you continue growing and getting outside of your comfort zone, you will grow in other areas as well. There will always be other things that can distract you away from what is important as your focus. As I tell my clients, the second you declare to take something on, it's like the universe conspires to get in the way. Something will show up and try to distract you.

This is where the rubber hits the road. How committed are you to this goal? How clear are you on the purpose of this goal? Is there something to let go of so you can pursue this goal? The 3 P's tool shown later in this chapter will help clarify the purpose of the goal that creates a powerful pull of motivation toward it. By getting focused, intentional and committed to the goal, we will find a way. We get what we are committed to.

**Persistence builds resilience**

Our oldest daughter has long been known for being stubborn. I didn't like the word stubborn. There can be a negative association with the word stubborn. What she absolutely has is persistence. When she gets her mind set on something, nothing stops her.

Going back to my Financial Peace University experience and that first class, I had hundreds of moments and opportunities where I wanted to quit. Resilience can be built. When you are facing self-doubt, negative talk, and yet you still are choosing to go ahead and do it anyway, this builds your resilience muscles.

In the brain an actual neurological associated resilience connection between the stimulus of doubt and the knowing a future success gets wired. When things become challenging and you continue trying even more new things, this resilience connection will push you farther and through to the other side.

### The wheel of life

You have already been introduced quickly to the wheel of life in chapter 2. This is one of the first tools I discovered in my coaching training. It was introduced quickly to get someone in crisis evaluated and headed in the right direction. I now want to expand on the value of it here.

I have seen many versions of it including a version for business. But the interesting thing about it is that it is so obviously simple and yet it shines some light onto what are some good areas that you might want to improve in. Opportunities for growth.

The tool forces us to zoom out of our "in the problem thinking" state and gets us to see the bigger picture of our life. The 10,000 foot view. It distinguishes obvious areas that are working and obvious areas that are not working. A client might want to do some coaching and not really know where they want to start. The wheel of life will point to possible areas for improvement and usually with detailed examples and evidence.

### Distract yourself in a healthy way

As mentioned in the chapter on relationships and releasing negative emotion, a possible healthy way is to distract yourself with self-development. Feel productive knowing that you are investing in yourself. You can either look at different areas in your life to improve or simply learn or do something new, something exciting, something out of your comfort zone. Consider a new language or hobby or new activity to join in on.

How do you feel when you learn something new? Personal growth can build confidence, stimulate creativity, and give us purpose in life. Maybe you already have a list of things you want to accomplish.

**Manufacture more motivation**

One of my challenges was not feeling motivated to do anything! Then I found this book titled "100 Ways To Motivate Yourself" by Steve Chandler. There were simple activities to try and at first, I was hesitant but I gave it a try. This lead me to doing stand-up comedy, starting a singles meetup group, and skydiving. I went from not feeling like brushing my teeth to feeling unstoppable.

Just a sample of some of the fun, get out of your own way motivation ideas include: get on your death bed, push all your own buttons, welcome the unexpected, light your lazy dynamite, get up on the right side, enjoy all your problems, keep changing your voice, go on a news fast, exploit your weakness and laugh for no reason. Each of the 100 challenges has a description explaining the assignment. I found myself looking forward to the next motivational challenge and the book got me off of my a$$.

The following are tools that will help you get to the purpose of something that is important to you, something that you want to accomplish. Why is that important? Knowing the purpose first sets up an invisible magnetic pull toward that goal. It sets up motivation to take you through to the goal even when you get off course. It gets to what is of value to you about the goal. And of course, values drive behavior ...

The 3 main tools are; S.M.A.R.T. Goals, The 3 P's and a Well-Formed Outcome or W.F.O. I encourage you to work through them.

Through that process there is something going on behind the scenes in your mind. Trust the structure, take action toward your goal and the goal/outcome is yours. Piece of cake!

**Get to the other side of comfortable**

To work on self-development is to expand and grow from where we have been to something bigger. Literally, the things that are holding you back is the comfort zone. If you wanted to do something and have not done it yet, it is probably because you are not comfortable with a new activity that you have never done before. If it were comfortable you would already be doing it ...right?

There is a coaching saying – get comfortable with being uncomfortable. Do something uncomfortable again and again and again and pretty soon you realize the fear is either numb, gone, or was never there in the first place. You have achieved the brain conditioning to being comfortable with being uncomfortable.

I set out to do all kinds of uncomfortable things. Run a marathon, become a coach, do stand-up comedy, public speaking, sky diving and this amusement ride that dropped you into a free fall from an extremely tall height. I took classical dancing lessons, taekwondo lessons, photography classes. I was so comfortable with being uncomfortable, committing to and trying new things, that I felt like I could do anything! Anything I said I was going to do, I would do.

I became more attractive. Not in a narcissistic way but people were absolutely fascinated with my unusual stories and gusto to try new things fearlessly. My personal growth developed personal relationships with friends I still have today. I actually consider myself and feel like an introvert and no one believes me.

**50 Goals exercise – what all do you want?**

Exercise of free hand goals, desires, and wants. Set a timer for 10 minutes. Imagine there is nothing to stop you from having or doing anything you want in life. You have a magic pen or pencil that allows you to have anything you want in life. Start the timer and go ...

Write out everything that you desire and want. Goals to accomplish. Places to see. Things to do. The perfect house. Any location in the world. Vacations. Health. Money. What makes you feel good? Who would you want to spend time with and where? What is something you have always wanted to do and now you can?

1. _____
2. _____
3. _____
4. _____
5. _____
6. _____
7. _____
8. _____
9. _____
10. _____
11. _____

## DIVORCE PARTY

12. _____
13. _____
14. _____
15. _____
16. _____
17. _____
18. _____
19. _____
20. _____
21. _____
22. _____
23. _____
24. _____
25. _____
26. _____
27. _____
28. _____
29. _____
30. _____
31. _____
32. _____

33. _____
34. _____
35. _____
36. _____
37. _____
38. _____
39. _____
40. _____
41. _____
42. _____
43. _____
44. _____
45. _____
46. _____
47. _____
48. _____
49. _____
50. _____

1. What is the ONE most meaningful of all these goals? Circle or star the absolute most important goal on this list.

2. Place an A next to the next most important goals on the list. And in order of significance and ranking value, place a B then C next to the remaining goals.

3. Go back to the A goals and write down next to them, what it will mean to you upon completing this goal?

**Design Your Future NOW!**

Now transfer the 50 goals above to the future, by when you want to have these goals accomplished below.

1 month

_____

_____

_____

_____

_____

3 months

_____

_____

_____

_____

_____

6 months

_____

_____

_____

_____

1 year

_____

_____

_____

_____

3 years

_____

_____

_____

_____

5 years

_____

_____

# DIVORCE PARTY

_____
_____
_____

10years

_____
_____
_____
_____

15 years

_____
_____
_____
_____

20 years

_____
_____
_____
_____

30 years

_____
_____
_____
_____

40 years

_____
_____
_____

50 years

_____
_____
_____
_____

End of Life – how do you want to be remembered and relationships

_____
_____
_____

## DIVORCE PARTY

1 year after-life

5 years after-life

10 years after-life

20 years after-life

_____

_____

_____

_____

Now take the ONE goal that was the absolute most significant goal and complete a SMART Goal in the next section.

### S.M.A.R.T. Goal Theory (Meyer, 2019)

So, what are S.M.A.R.T goals? S.M.A.R.T is an acronym.

S is specific, must be detailed with a plan.

M is measurable, able to be measured and known.

A is aligned, must be aligned with your purpose and vision.

R is for risky, must be a stretch or a risk.

T is for time-based, must be completed by a certain time.

On a side note, this is one of three of my favorite goal tools. The first one, of course, is the three P's that I use all the time. The next one is the well-formed outcome or W.F.O., which is basically a S.M.A.R.T goal except expanded. And then the S.M.A.R.T goal that is the quick and dirty of the W.F.O.

When would you use a S.M.A.R.T goal? Similar to the three P's, anytime that I have a project that just feels overwhelming, S.M.A.R.T goals is a really great tool to develop that goal. There's a saying that we can't achieve a goal that we don't see. And another saying, that everything that has been created has been created twice.

The streets in a city, they didn't just appear. Somebody actually had to see those streets in their mind. And maybe even longer before that, maybe there were trails or paths through the woods or the country. And it was seen as, "This is a useful path," but somebody had to have that vision. You can't create something that you don't know, something that you can't envision.

As soon as you have the vision, then you are able to do the second part, which is actually make that vision come into existence. So, the very first thing that you want to do is state specifically what the is, "My goal" is and then explain it.

It is important that you think this goal in the future in the present tense. So, what do I mean by that? Well, if I was wanting to start an exercise program, I want to state that goal as, "I have started an exercise program and am already feeling the benefits." It's stated in the present tense as if it's already happening or already true. And also, you want to attach to that goal, the date that it is to be completed.

**S – Specific.** I know from coaching clients that when something is out of somebody's comfort zone, even just stating the goal sometimes can be uncomfortable. And so for this whole process with these S.M.A.R.T goals, I really want to encourage you to look at these as if, "I'm just writing these down as an observer." Let go of the how you are going to complete this and just get down to the details of exactly what it is that you value and are wanting to accomplish.

The reason this is important is that I see all the time some incredible coaches and some incredible people that are in NLP or hypnosis, and I see that they are so incredibly talented. And sometimes I even feel a little envious that I don't have those skills, whether it's being able to just naturally do a process or just their personalities. Being very charismatic that is an attractive quality.

And what blows my mind is that so often a lot of these incredibly talented people never have the courage to just state what it is that they want and their goals. I see these people 10 years later and wow, the ones who seemed so over-the-top amazingly talented, they have left the playing field. They are out of doing change work. I thought for sure these would be the ones to be so successful and on top. They appeared to me that they were the leaders of the pack. But without courage to declare to the universe what we want it will never happen.

Goals are that way ... the idea comes fast and has to be acted upon quickly. The goals come and go quickly and wait for you to capture them. Otherwise, the un-stated goals, dreams, and opportunities, drift away with certainty. They move onto someone else who is ready and has the courage to claim them as theirs. Leap and the net will appear.

I really want to encourage you to let go of how this is all going to happen. There's something magical, there's something so magical that happens. And this, of course, leads back into the law of attraction. Here's an example: when you get a new car and all of a sudden you see that same car in your neighborhood. You've never seen it before, ever, and then all of a sudden there's 20 of them driving by your house. Will you attract circumstances and opportunities that support your goal? The opportunities were always there, but now that you have gotten clarity on your goals, you will be amazed how much appears and comes to you in opportunities, paths, and doors that open for you.

**M – Measurable.** It's real important that you're able to measure it, because if you do not have a way to measure it, what evidence do you have that you're moving toward or away from this goal? I was coaching somebody one time, back when I was running marathons. He wanted some coaching from me for running a half marathon and he some came up with some specific measurable goals. And what was interesting is, after he not only accomplished his goals but exceeded all them, he was upset that he saw that others had done more than he did. He had stopped at the half marathon and he was upset with himself that there were others that continued on and did the full marathon.

Well, what I know is that if you train for a half marathon, you're going to run a half marathon. If you don't train for a full marathon, it's just not going to happen. He was not clear enough with what it was he was specifically wanted to get out of this goal. And to be accountable as a coach, I didn't see that. However, we then had this opportunity to look at, "What was it that you were really trying to achieve? What stopped you from wanting more?" And that actually turned into a really powerful session where was able to dig into some truly deep stuff going back to when he was a kid.

I asked him, "Where else is it in your life have you exceeded your expectations, accomplished your goals and yet, are still not happy with your results?" His head dropped at the realization of a behavior pattern he had been doing his entire life. It was like a powerful punch to his gut as it hit. His anger state went to calmness. His rapid speech slowed down. His higher pitch voice lowered deeply. His goal wasn't about going a distance or even beating someone else. How long has this been going on? No matter how hard he tried when he was a child, it was never good enough. His goal *specifically* was about a powerful desire to receive approval, from someone that was not even there.

**A – Aligned** Your goal must be aligned with your purpose and vision. This is for ecology around all of and throughout your life. How is this going to affect myself, relationships, my environment, and my identity? What if this goal is a contradiction or conflicts with your purpose, and your vision, and your values? This will probably interfere with your accomplishing this goal and not be settled until you ask this question, "Is this something that actually supports my purpose? Is this something that supports my vision? Is this something I even want to do? What do I get out of it?" It's real important that you get aligned with that.

I'm sure you've all experienced that Christmas morning, you get that toy that you had to have and then five minutes later it feels worthless. It doesn't feel like it means anything. So, reaching your goal, it's really important that this goal is in alignment with your bigger purpose and your bigger vision.

**R - Risky.** It must be a stretch or a risk. It's so important that we are willing to stretch outside of our comfort zone. I was in a training where we all had to come up with something that was outside of our comfort zone so we could understand that feeling, that fear that will show up in our clients when we do something uncomfortable. Different people chose different things that challenged them. One was learning a language. One of them was demonstrating Tai Chi. One was to learn photography. One was to play an instrument. What I chose, and I even get anxious thinking about it, was to do stand-up comedy, which terrifies the hell out of me. And I did it. That was my stretch, and I went to Chicago and took some comedy classes. I went to Indianapolis and took some improv classes. I bought different CDs, books, and DVDs, and really put a lot of work into this two-minutes that I was up on stage and it felt like six hours. And people laughed. They laughed at me, they laughed with me. And it was incredible.

But the most important thing is what I got out of it, well, for the coaching training, was how it feels to do something when you're uncomfortable. And there's something powerful about stretching outside of your comfort zone. Because all the things that you have not gotten, that you've wanted to get, are outside of your comfort zone.

Plain and simple, if it was comfortable, you'd be doing it already. It's important that this be something that is uncomfortable to you because you get to grow. You get to stretch, and you get to grow from that, as well as build confidence that, "Hey, I'm able to do this. I thought it felt like it was impossible, it felt like it was unattainable, and yet I did it." And how cool is that to build up your self-esteem and your confidence about taking on things that are outside of your comfort zone simply by taking on that challenge.

And here's the thing again, it's so important to mention that we let go of how this is going to happen. I am not saying you don't have to do anything, but obviously you will. Most important of all is that we're just continually building this confidence, to stretch ourselves outside of our comfort zone and trust the process. There's so much more of life that we may be missing out on because, on an unconscious level, we're afraid to even try to put our foot outside of our comfort zone. I really want to encourage you to take on something that's risky that supports you.

**T – Time-based.** The last letter in the acronym is T, and that's time-based. It must be completed by a certain time. There's something fascinating when we set a goal, and this is called cognitive dissonance, when we set a goal that is outside of where we are and who we are outside of ourselves. And it's something that we presently don't have. For example, for me it was marathon running. And to just say that I'm going to run a marathon ... I remember the first time I said that, I went into my office and I knew it was important for me to make it real. And I knew that if I had the confidence to go into my office and announce I was going to run a marathon, that it was becoming real to me. And again, there's this uncomfortableness with being willing to even say it to yourself, let alone to say it in public.

Long story short, I went into my office and said, "I'm going to run marathon." And it was quiet. And then everyone burst into laughter, because at that time I was really overweight, and the thought of being able to run a marathon, it seemed ridiculous to everybody in the office. I remember feeling hurt, and yet I also knew that it was important for me to stretch outside of my comfort zone. And so, with having a certain time to accomplish this goal, set up an additional cognitive dissonance, where you are now, and where you want to be.

It's so important that you make this goal real as opposed to ... someday maybe. If you don't put a date and time on this, it's not really a goal. It's just kind of wishing and hoping. And of course, that's actually a barrier to performance. When you wish and you hope, that is the language of a *barrier to performance*. If I wish this happened or I hope this happens, it's just not going to happen. That's actually stating you're not doing it, right? So it's when you start to get crystal clear about this goal and speak about it in the present tense already, go to the future to speak about it into the present tense, it becomes real and your unconscious mind is listening.

I hope you use enjoy S.M.A.R.T goals. It's a powerful tool and simple tool to just really get clear about what it is that you're wanting to accomplish and ways that will support you to motivate yourself to complete it.

Pick one thing you want to work on with your personal growth and development and fill out a S.M.A.R.T. Goal below.

**Self Development - S.M.A.R.T Goal (Meyer, 2019)**

**What is the Goal?** (Written in the future tense as if already achieved)

_____

_____

_____

**S - Specific.**

What will the goal accomplish?

_____

_____

_____

How and why will it be accomplished?

_____

_____

_____

**M - Measurable.**

How will you measure whether or not the goal has been reached (list at least two indicators)?

_____

_____

**A - Achievable.**

Is it possible?

_____

_____

Have others done it successfully?

_____

_____

Do you have the necessary knowledge, skills, abilities, and resources to accomplish the goal?

_____

_____

Will meeting the goal challenge you without defeating you?

_____

_____

_____

### R - Results-focused.

What is the reason, purpose, or benefit of accomplishing the goal?

_____

_____

_____

What is the outcome result (not the activities leading up to the result) of the goal?

_____

_____

_____

### T - Time-based.

What is the established completion date and does that completion date create a practical sense of urgency?

_____

_____

_____

Revised Goal:

_____

_____

_____

_____

_____

### The 3 P's

*Purpose, Products and Process*

What are the three P's? Why and when would you use them? Three P's stands for purpose, products, and process. If you have an upcoming project or goal that seems overwhelming, the three P's is a powerful tool to chunk down something big into small pieces that feel and look absolutely achievable. The three P's will also clarify your vision and identify the underlying purpose. And lastly, when you get your outcomes, they are in rapport with your values, and values drive your behaviors.

The first P is purpose. The purpose is the why are you going after this. Zoom out and way up above yourself to a 10,000 foot view. How does achieving this goal get you what you want? What's in it for you? Zoom out again and ask yourself, what does that get you? Have you ever achieved the goal and it felt empty? When you accomplished your goal, it was not how you thought it would feel. Why?

We want to write the three P's down on a piece of paper and speak them out loud as we get them. This activates your minds VAK - visual, auditory, and kinesthetic. The purpose is usually the shortest of the three P's. It should not be more than one or two sentences long, do not think about this very long, just a couple minutes.

Brian Tracy said that, "Successful people decide things quickly and change their minds slowly. While unsuccessful people decide slowly and change their minds quickly." The purpose of the first P is to set up a powerful magnetic pull that is in alignment with your values. Your behaviors act out your values on an unconscious level before you are even conscious of it. A purpose statement might look like this: the purpose of this goal is to improve the quality of my life and my family's.

The second P is products or outcomes. The products are "what" you get. These are the milestones of your action steps. This helps create boundaries and sharp focus; distinctions that measure whether you are moving toward or away from your purpose and goal. A person wanting to run a 5k may have these products; to not get injured and to be safe, to finish the race, to have a personal best time, and to recover from the race easily and feel good. Products are your evidence so you can celebrate or learn from being curious about what happened instead. Remember the presupposition that; "there is no failure, only feedback".

The third P is process. Napoleon Hill said "Action is the real measure of intelligence." The process is the sequential action steps used to move you toward and fulfill the purpose. This is chunking down the big thing into actionable steps. If an action step seems too overwhelming, chunk it down till it absolutely feels achievable.

Include everything from beginning to end don't focus on the how it will happen but just what needs to happen. Imagine that there is nothing you can't achieve. All you have to do is write it down.

I hope you enjoyed learning about the three P's next time you have something that looks feels or sounds overwhelming. Give the three Ps a try!

## The 3 P's Form

**P – Purpose** (a simple sentence or two about what this goal gets you)

_____

_____

_____

**P – Products** (the outcomes and what evidence you want to produce / manifest both in the world, others and within yourself. What will you see, hear and feel?)

_____

_____

_____

_____

_____

**P – Process** – (the action steps written down in sequential order)

_____

_____

_____

_____

_____

_____

## WFO – Well-Formed Outcome

(O'Conner & Seymour, 2011) The WFO is like the SMART goal but expanded. I look at the SMART goals as the quick and dirty but larger projects can benefit from the expanded depth of the WFO.

## WFO - Clarity

What do you want?

_____

_____

_____

Can it be initiated by you?

_____

_____

_____

Can it be controlled by you?

_____

_____

_____

Is it large or manageable?

_____

_____

_____

Chunk down if necessary.

_____
_____
_____

**WFO – Evidence**

How will you know when you have it?

_____
_____
_____

What will you see?

_____
_____
_____

What will you hear?

_____
_____
_____

How will you feel?

_____
_____
_____

What might you smell or taste?

_____

_____

_____

What will be different now that you have it?

_____

_____

_____

**WFO – Context**

Where does it fit in your life?

_____

_____

_____

When do you want it?

_____

_____

_____

Where do you want it?

_____

_____

_____

With whom do you want it?

_____

_____

_____

Under what circumstances do you want it?

_____

_____

_____

**WFO – Other Considerations**

What else in your life will be impacted?

_____

_____

_____

What positive and negative consequences may be created?

Positive –

_____

_____

_____

Negative –

_____

_____

# DIVORCE PARTY

What resources do you have?

_____

_____

_____

What resources do you need?

_____

_____

_____

What are you already doing?

_____

_____

_____

What will achieving this outcome do for you?

_____

_____

_____

_____

_____

## WFO – Taking Action

How do you plan to be in action?

_____
_____
_____

Is there more than one way?

_____
_____
_____

What are they?

_____
_____
_____

What are your time frames?

_____
_____

What stops you?

_____
_____
_____

How will you celebrate your success and learning?

## WFO – Looking Ahead

What do you see in the future?

Step into the future having achieved the outcome.

Describe how it feels.

Reflect back on how you achieved the outcome.

What supported you?

_____

_____

_____

Did anything get in the way?

_____

_____

_____

What might you do differently?

_____

_____

_____

**Learning moving forward**

We never stop learning. Until our last breath, we are learning.

Tony Robbins (Robbins, 1994) uses an acronym for this never-ending improvement. C.A.N.I. – Constant and Never-Ending Improvement. This originates from the Japanese word *kaizen* meaning "change for better," without inherent meaning of either "continuous" or "philosophy." In simple terms, *kaizen* is the philosophy and science of constant and never-ending improvement or betterment or refinement. It is the idea that nothing is ever finished, or declared perfect; there is always room for improvement.

## Edward Deming - The Kaizen Principle

### Continued Self-development

The Edward Deming principle significantly outlines quality over quantity. He invented a practice that iteratively improved quantity over time. This principle however is known as Kaizen in Japanese. Kaizen values the very little things of improvement, everything counts, little progress all sum up to higher quality. Kaizen means continued improvement. The concept ensures that it was everyone's duty to continually make incremental progress, improvement in every area.

Edward Deming born October 14, 2019 developed this principle just immediately after the devastating effects and end of the WW11 in Japan. He was one of the few persons sent from America to develop and help the country stand again from the rumbles of the war. And today, the result of the Deming principle can be easily seen. Japan has developed its economy through superior technology products and are also one of the leading countries in manufacturing.

Although Edward Deming died December 1993, he received the country's highest civilian award before his death. He's principle however left a large foot print on almost every production and manufacturing industry in Japan as well as other adopting sectors.

For instance, when practiced in a manufacturing industry, the Kaizen concepts proposes that it is everyone's job to constantly seek ways to improve everything they get involved in. A factory worker would halt his work and show a fellow worker how to make proper corrections to a design or an effective method for production. This little change and advise on how to perform better would sum up in the overall and output of the industry. Quality in this context may mean, more quality output at improved production time.

One might say that Japan already had a reputation for craftsmanship and detailed production techniques prior to Deming. That's true, of course, but Deming-initiated improvements allowed Japanese companies to slowly but surely creep past Western countries in quality of modern manufacturing process, supply chain, and cost of production.

**Keynotes From Edward Deming's principle.**

From the Kaizen principle, a number of important lessons can be pulled out.

**Changes takes place in an iterative way:** Deming principle always reintegrate the need for progressive changes and also incremental development of one's ability. Only through this would you be able to achieve the topmost quality of whatever goal you might be working towards. Rather than big moves, or exaggerated changes, development comes through an iterative process over time.

**Little things count:** Like every success story been told, the epilogue usually start with, "the journey of a thousand miles begins with a step. Kaizen emphasizes that for every progress or change, some little improvement has taken place. However little, every improvement counts.

**Quality is superior to quantity:** Edward Deming taught that aiming towards quantity is important than every other thing. This principle emphasizes iterative development of quality. In Japan, manufacturing industries who followed the practice have continually dominated the marketplace.

How does this apply to you? Having just a little quality time of reading or any self-development practice is one step ahead than long hours of ineffectiveness chased by lack of concentration or mindfulness to work any other activities involved.

**Practice makes perfect:** from the Deming's principle, we can easily conclude that to achieve quality, lots of minute, iterative process was placed together. While Edward Deming was engaging the Kaizen principle with the Japanese, as at the time of non-technological advancement and war depleted States with virtually nothing, he enlightened that for progress to be made, and to achieve quality, you only have to get better at what you do. This highlights the importance of practice.

Keep practicing for self-improvements, to improve quality. However, just as pointed out before, even while genuinely practicing improving yourself, it is important to note that every little effort leads to noticeable progress and continued motivation.

**Kaizen teaches focus:** To achieve anything worth note, focus is expedient. Kaizen involves participation and active incorporation of the brainpower and intrinsic ability of individuals to achieve success. These is also an associated concept of Kaizen that teaches the idea and importance of scheduled, super focuses period of attention to a single process. The process can be defined in any context, whether as self-development, production process or work.

Edward taught that a focus of attention on a particular activity would in a short period of time, definitely bring success. Success could mean, superior quality of an output of a production process, achieving personal and self set goals etc. Focus is key to improvement in Kaizen.

Edward Deming developed a cycle known as the Deming cycle: Plan, Do, Check and Act. Here's is what the cycles refers to.

**<u>Plan.</u>**

To achieve anything, Deming taught that you must first come up with a plan. You need to plan by analyzing the core problem requiring a solution, the process and method for fixing such problem and the resources required. Thus it can be applied to day to day life and self-development process. You need to plan by setting goals and ways in which you can achieve these goals.

The next thing after planning is to take action.

**<u>Do.</u>**

After plans has been made, you need to get to work. Edward taught that only the plans made should be put to action. Production industries that have outlined their plans according to the Deming cycle, stuck solely to it. The rules are, Do everything in the plan and don't do anything that's not in your plans.

As an individual trying to achieve a goal or self-development objectives, you should lay out plans and completely put them to action.

**<u>Study and check your actions to the plans listed.</u>**

Deming taught the Japanese companies that no matter the progress made, there is always need to constantly study the actions and plans. Cross checking you actions and plans would help you see better ways to achieve your objectives and also see if the expected results are achieved.

**Act.**

Act by reacting to results achieved by implementing the plan. This involved checking the results and seeking ways to make any necessary adjustment that maybe required.

This is the Deming cycle. It is however better to repeat this cycle to ensure continued motivation for self-improvements.

**How little improvement over time creates excellence.**

The Deming principle can be applied to your daily lives and development. In the quest to get better, you should be mindful of the amount of efforts you put to achieve your goals. It might be easy to make wishful aims of getting better or achieving a goal without putting in any amount of efforts. But this is a violation of the Deming principles which states you must plan, carry out actions, study your actions against plans before acting.

What are your goals? What do you wish to achieve? What plans have you made to achieve these plans? So, you wish to achieve success? These questions are important to your desire of excellence and self-development.

The Edward Deming principle will help you achieve this. Kaizen states that with little improvement and continuous incremental development, success would be achieved in exponentially less time.

Big things start little. Constant little things would sum up to a large output and outburst of success. The rule of success attained through little efforts sustained over time states that a multiplier effect is obtained on all little efforts directed toward excellence or self-development and this leads to success in a shirt time.

### How to remain motivated to achieve success with constant little improvement.

There's are rules to achieving any form of success. However, some set of rules are meant to be followed for success from constant effort directed towards improvement and self-development.

**Set plans-** just like as discussed in the Deming cycle, for any desired level of success, you need to set goals, write them down. Questions like what do you want to achieve? How you wish to achieve these plans should be clearly stated in the plans.

**Start right away and be focused** - a philosophy for thinking and winning states that, if you are going to do anything; do it right away. To achieve success through little and constant development, you need to start acting on your plans and be focused. In kaizen, a scheduled super focused period of attention is directed on a single activity to achieve quality success. Therefore, to achieve excellence with little effort over time, you need to be focused.

**Once you start, never give up-** once you start working towards excellence or any self-development goal, never give up. However, with reference to the Deming cycle, you need to constantly check and study your plans and actions and see how to constantly improve and act.

**Keep improving productivity by constantly improving your efforts** - from the Deming cycle, you act after studying your plans and actions. This is where you improve your efforts, re-strategize how you wish to achieve self-development.

Keep going at your goal of self-development. Never back down. Every little effort counts, and all little things count. Once you feel you already achieved your goal of excellence, raise the bar and increase the standard of goals again. Just like Japan, through the teaching of Edward Deming still keep improving their economy and technological prowess as leading top world countries.

This same principle can be used for continuous growth and motivation for overall self-development.

**Apply the Kaizen principle.**

The kaizen principle of continuous improvement would get you to achieve continued self-development. Self-improvements would place you at the peak, however, you do not stop, the kaizen principle discourages halt of developmental process.

**Continuous changes-** the world never ends developing and improving, either economically or technologically, you can continue developing yourself also.

**The dangers of not constantly improving.**

A worse thing than being stagnant is not growing and improving. Once you don't improve, the world at that moment seems to have ended. Decline sets in, and with that, the world passes you up. Consider the technological prowess of the Japanese industry who constantly used the Edward Deming Kaizen principle; these industries have taken over major markets of technological demands. The economy of the county is on a steady rise, that's what constant growth produce; strive for continuous send development.

It would be essential to ask where the previous leading industries are today, and why they were dethroned. The answers would not be too far-fetched; they didn't grow, they went into a decline and the world has moved passed them.

The world keeps moving, constant development and a high pace advancement; the question is how do you match this? Keep moving, keep developing yourself

Here are questions to answer; do you want to escape developmental decline? Do you want to remain at the peak? Then, always improve yourself, in which ever little way, it counts long term.

**Lack of continued self-development would cause the following-**

**Developmental Decline-** absence of continued self-development would lead to a sharp decline.

**The world moves passed you-** look out and see some mistakes made by fallen giants in any business, production, entertainment or technological sectors. They never work on improving themselves, no matter how little. Consequently, they went into a decline and the world moved passed them.

As an individual, this shouldn't become your fate. Pick yourself up and constantly work on self-development.

**It becomes harder to motivate yourself to achieve greatness-** once you fail to develop yourself, it gets difficult to set goals and consequently achieve success. Turning it around can be done with more effort in creating inertia.

Self-improvements should be a daily lifestyle. It may however, be challenging to remain on a routine or stay on the oath of continued self-development; distractions, loss of concentration, focus and also lack of interest, may set in. But it is your duty to never let that get in your way.

Remember the Kaizen principle, start little, grow and get better, that way you would be able to constantly motivate yourself for continuous self-development.

Notes:

_____

_____

_____

_____

_____

_____

_____

_____

_____

_____

_____

_____

_____

_____

_____

# Chapter 8
## Environment

"When a flower doesn't bloom, you fix the environment in which it grows, not the flower." - Alexander Den Heijer

**What you will get in this chapter**

✓ Procrastination – bust, shred, slice and eating frogs

✓ Get fired up on organizing

✓ "A place for everything and everything in its place"

✓ 3 types of storage

✓ Organize your mind with laser focus!

✓ Organize your environment space!

✓ Making highly effective To Do Today lists

✓ How do you want your HOME environment to feel?

✓ Home environment S.M.A.R.T. goals

✓ How do you want your WORK environment to feel?

✓ Work Environment S.M.A.R.T. goals

When I first learned about the wheel of life, it didn't seem like the environment was significant enough to me to be one of the eight key areas of everyone's lives. Sometimes we can be so close to a problem that we can't see we are in it, or that there is something better outside of it.

If you listen to someone talking about any problem, it seems they are fully in trance with the problem. Simply shifting someone's focus with questions outside of the problem, "what do they want instead of the problem," blows the walls out of the problem. The problem is not the problem. The problem is not focusing outside of the problem, "what do you want instead?"

Our environments shapes and have a significant effect on our quality of life, whether we want it to or not, whether we are aware of it or not. The awesome news is that when you focus on how do you want your environment to look, feel, and sound like instead, amazingly we become aware of all the resources that are literally already in our lap. We shift from being at effect of the world to being at cause of our life.

Our environment includes: everything outside of ourselves internally, although our environments will affect our internal experience positively or negatively. Your environments include: where, when, and with whom are your behaviors seen?

### Procrastination – bust, shred, slice and eating frogs

For me personally, procrastination was my challenge when it came to doing something with my home environment. And if you have "piles of things" whether it is envelopes, unfinished projects, paperwork, lists, clutter in a drawer, garage, or attic, there is hope! A pile of things that are not in their place is really a pile of decisions that have not been made.

An excellent book and enjoyable read on procrastination is "Eat That Frog" by Brian Tracy. (Tracy, 2002) If you ever get around to it (see what I did there?) it turns putting things off into a variety of fascinating ways to bust through putting things off. And offers 21 different ways to move forward through procrastination.

It almost seems like procrastination is a side effect of not being interested enough in the organization or doing things. This book is full of 21 different angles of attack that are fascinating and even fun! There are a handful of books I will reread multiple times. This is definitely one of those books that are worth reading again and again to brush up on being an action-oriented person.

The first method, of course, is to take on the frog. Eat That Frog! What is the ugliest thing on your To Do list today? That thing that has you triathlete Olympians committed and busy doing the un-important things to unconsciously avoid what is important and needs to be done? Eat that frog first and you will feel awesome and motivated to knock out the rest of the list! Imagine how it will feel after that thing is in the past and complete. Lighter? Fulfilled? Proud? Peaceful?

In his book – "First Things First," – Steven Covey (Covey, 1995) discusses the value of doing what is important first. We often are busy with the non-significant in our lives, all in an attempt to avoid the important and significant things in our lives. Take care of the big rocks in your life and the little rocks will all fit in and fall in place naturally.

One of my favorite taking-actions of moving forward methods of Brian's is Swiss cheesing. If you have a big project or a BIG FROG, if the next step feels overwhelming and TOO much, it may need to be chunked down into smaller baby bites.

That big solid block of cheese is actually made up of several or smaller ingredients and baby steps. What is an action that you can take that is chunked down so small that you are absolutely guaranteed success? Maybe making the appointment can be broken down into a guaranteed step like Googling their website while you are sitting on the toilet. Make it so and flush that baby step into the past!

It can be more important to have success at doing little things that motivate you to keep going. The brain drops feel fabulous dopamine into the pleasure center of your brain. Get addicted being successful, taking action, becoming confident that you absolutely can do what you declare out into the world!

**Get fired up on organizing**

If our environment is not working for us, it is natural and easy to focus on the problem. Instead, we want to focus outside of the problem. What do we want instead? Getting clarity on what the 'what' is starts the process of manifesting the acquiring of what we want instead.

Not being organized in our environment not only clutters our physical realm, but it clutters our thoughts. If we need to sit down at the table and make a To Do list and the table is covered with clutter and the surface is buried, how does that feel? I remember being so pissed with my mess that I created, I took my arm like it was a windshield wiper blade and wiped off 12" of clutter on the dining table, crashing it all onto the floor.

Ahhhhhhhhhhhh finally! A clean space I can work from. It felt wonderful! I know could see my thoughts and feel I had a space to start organizing. And deciding what to do with the crap on the floor became easy when I realized I just need to make 3 decisions, where everything goes.

**"A place for everything and everything in it's place."**

I used to hate that saying. I thought what kind of sick freak would obsessively control their lives that way? Then needlepoint the quote and frame it for all who visit their sick freak-clean organized house to see! Geeshhh, who even does that or has the time to pick up needle pointing as a hobby or would even enjoy needle pointing? There is no freedom in all of that, I thought.

Turns out they were on to something. In his book – "Getting Things Done" by David Allen (Allen, 2015), my eyes were opened to the awesome and powerful value of that quote. I was getting in my own way of being organized with some limiting beliefs I had about what being organized would look like. G.T.D. is another amazing must-read book and on my must-reread list of favorite books.

I have always been a list person and that does not mean at all that I am effective with organization. You might think how can that be? Believe it or not, if you are not a list person, or good at making lists, it is possible to be really good at doing nothing and instead accumulating notebooks full of lists. Perhaps a form of hording?

Making lists and being busy organizing notes is not the same as organizing your inner and outer world or taking action. Or continually going to school but not applying yourself with that knowledge, getting employment and working. Or going through training after training after trainings, and not starting a business or using the knowledge. A form of piling up and preparing to have courage one day, maybe ... Being busy is not the same as being productive. We can fool ourselves into thinking we are productive by burying ourselves in the 3p's of not taking action – paperwork, policies, and procedures. Creating, producing, accumulating, and crop-dusting others with our genius paperwork, emails, rules, policies, and procedures with the hopes to appear we are important, busy or productive. But are we actually wanting to look good to ourselves or others by procrastinating, limiting, hindering, stunting or paralyzing ourselves or others and not efficiently getting things done? Busy doing nothing. In our personal life, we get to choose what we do and the actions we take to get organized and be productive.

"Action is the real measure of intelligence."

- *Napoleon Hill* (Hill, 1937)

## 3   types of storage

There are 3 environment spaces we create with organization.

1. Primary value storage space

2. Secondary value storage space

3. Archival storage space

If it doesn't fit in these 3 spaces, throw it away. If your butt is puckering at the thought of throwing something away that you never use, because a part of you feels it has value, give it away or set it on the curb. If no one picks it up by garbage day, well maybe it is trash.

**Organize your mind with laser focus!**

If you don't know where to start, start anywhere, start exactly where you are. After I windshield wiped my dining table off with my windshield wiper arm, I proudly sat down at my clean table. It felt pretty damn good actually, now having a clean space. Despite the chaos on the floor, and things still rolling around the kitchen and into the living room, as my cat ran into the kitchen wondering what the hell was going on.

I took a deep, deep breath of fresh air and let it out twice as slowly. I took another deep breath of nourishing oxygen and held it for a moment, and let it out twice as slowly. I had a brand-new notebook and my favorite pen and I started to simply capture all the known loose ends in my life that I needed to write down or possibly would forget something important.

Just like that table and the mess on the floor, my thoughts are similar to the 3 storage areas. I want to capture them all in 1 central storage place so I remember what is important. And capture them however possible so I can transfer them to a central location I can visit.

a. High value mind storage space – We can only focus on 7 +/- 2 things at any one time. If our mind is a turbulent hurricane of things to do, we will be in fight/flight/freeze mode; reacting instead of choosing what to do. We have to create a clean table space in our mind; create a way to organize our mind with automation and extra memory. Similar to an external hard drive storage space so that we can take a deep breath and let it out twice as slowly, and begin to enjoy life. If we are always worried about what we are forgetting that is urgent, we are not focusing on appreciating life and being grateful for what and who we have in our life now. We must act on the things to do now, the important and urgent. What to do today, this week, or has a deadline, expiration, potentially affects you and your happiness. If there are things that can be automated, make that happen with phone reminders, calendars, and auto bill pay. Set HAVE-TO-DO or H.T.D. trip wires by placing them on your todays to do list, that you keep on your phone or a small pad of paper in your pocket. Review and be committed to look at this list throughout the day, and take action on the list.

b. Less value mind storage space – things you need to do tomorrow or in the future that are date dependent or urgent. Set it and forget it. Schedule future oil changes in the future. Not critical today, but HIGHLY important and critical in 3 months or 3000 miles from last oil change. Capture all these important things to do. Everything outside of daily focus and short-term memory to do today. Throw their importance into the future in a way that will create confidence and trust with automated trip wires. Thank goodness for smart phones, computers, and reminders. How often are we worried about things are going to happen and we forgot about what is important to do today? That is a waste of our 7 +/- 2 pieces of information we can focus on and take action on. Free up your focus and take control of your effectiveness by storing things for tomorrow into technology, reminders, and automation.

c. Archival mind storage space – sometimes we get caught up into the chaos of now and escape by daydreaming. If you have ever heard the negative expression about someone who always has their head in the clouds, or that they are not a realist but a dreamer, the accuser might be thinking of this person in that context of avoiding the important. I am not saying that dreaming is wasteful time unless it is used to escape dealing with something important. This can become an addictive behavior where the mind drops dopamine into the pleasure center of the brain and reinforces the negative behavior by reinforcing when you feel pain and triggering an escape behavior. What is important should never be sacrificed for what is least important. If you are escaping doing something urgent right now by avoiding it, then that reality is not a working scenario long-term. How do you become a healthy dreamer? I get totally excited about the future and it motivates me to stay on top of my mind's organization to get things done. What things do you want to do in the future that ignite your passion? What hobbies, interests, activities, trainings classes, and goals are on your bucket list or life purpose? We can store these things as a note in a journal or, even easier, on your phone. Get creative and create a vision board and post it in a place where you will see it all the time. This will remind you of what is coming up for you as a reward for being organized with your mind and taking action toward living out your dreams. Always knowing you can return to visit, to get excited about the future or start something in an instant when you have free time.

**Organize your environment space**

It is worth repeating ... There are 3 environments we create with organization.

1. Primary value storage space

2. Secondary value storage space

3. Archival value storage space

If it doesn't fit in these 3 spaces, throw it away. If your butt is puckering at the thought of throwing something away that you never use, because a part of you feels it has value, give it away or set it on the curb. If no one picks it up by garbage day, well maybe it is trash.

So, back to my kitchen table story. I had a notepad that collected all my thoughts of what was important. I was feeling highly motivated, like my batteries had been recharged. Interesting how clutter drains our batteries. As the clutter left, my energy level increased!

Looking down at the mess on the floor, next I then began the process of organizing my physical space. I grabbed a garbage can and put it next to me at the table, and started sorting everything into 3 piles.

**Rule number 1.** - Sort everything into 3 piles; a) do today, b) deal with soon, and c) archive or store in file cabinet. And if it doesn't fit in the first 3 piles, throw it away. Quickly I had organized 3 piles on my dining room table.

Eventually this paper management and sorting system turned into an office inbox and office storage. Everything that came in the house like bills, notices, paperwork, business-related items, business cards, important mail, everything went straight into the inbox. It had a place that was organized. Regardless of how busy I was, it at least had an organized place to land. Then later, by the end of the day I would empty and sort the inbox and take action if I could, use file storage or calendar schedule.

**Rule number 2.** - If you can deal with it in 2 minutes or less, do it immediately. Back then I was using a paper scheduler. This particular fancy kind had a monthly, weekly, and daily planner marked with 15-minute daily increments. This became my to-do list for today and the future. As the pages turned with a new day and my attention was drawn to today's schedule, there were things that were scheduled from the past that would show up on my today's to-do schedule list.

The nice thing with the scheduler was that there was only one time slot available for anything. This kept me from double scheduling a time slot. I would always check first before making any time commitment. I eventually learned it was worth glancing at the next day's schedule to peek into my time commitment and would plan on enough time to keep early appointments or appointments requiring longer travel.

This same 3 level storage space concept then moved to my kitchen.

1. Prime – Counter space.

2. Secondary – Shelves.

3. Archival – Lower, back space cabinets, hard to get to spaces.

Archival, you know where you store that fondue set and mini donut factory machine that someone gave you as a gift. And what about all the kitchen drawer gadgets? If you haven't used it in a year, throw it away or give it to the curbside charity.

I would then repeat this process room-by-room and space-by-space. Every space in my life, including drawers, shelves, cabinets, and all physical spaces would receive the same organization. Every hiding catch-all space was in my cross hairs to integrate and Cyborg into my new way of thinking. It was pretty freaking exhilarating. It felt wonderful! I looked forward to my organized space; that felt amazing. In a way, I felt like I had grown up in so many ways.

### Making highly effective To-Do Today lists

I have always been a list person. I became so good at it I created all sorts of lists. Eventually what was important got lost in the piles of lists. The most important list you want to have is the To-Do list for today. Want to know a powerful way to make this list highly effective? When you write down an item on the list ask yourself this – is this one step or is this something bigger that can be broken down into a sequence of smaller steps? AND here is the big bang that will transform your organization life, write down the answer to: "what is the next step I can do?"

Write your list with action steps. Knowing what is the next action step is powerful and here is why. A simple thing like getting your brake pads changed is not just 1 item on the list. Can it be broken down into smaller steps? Absolutely YES!

You might need to: Schedule the time to go. Schedule the appointment. Are they open when you want to go? Do you have money in your account? What does the repair cost or do you need to get a quote first? Can you wait or do you need a ride? How long will it take?

There are lots of things to consider, but most importantly, what is the next action step to make? The way our minds work, if we have more than one thing to decide, we go into analysis paralysis and may not even be aware of it consciously. These are the items that get put off and procrastinated because of unconscious indecisiveness. By considering fully what is needed to plan the goal, and seeing what the next logical action step is, we free our mind up to plan out our to do today list with confidence and success.

**How do you want your HOME environment to feel?**

How would you rank your home environment Negative, neutral or positive experience and circle a number on the scale.

-10 -9 -8 -7 -6 -5 -4 -3 -2 -1 0 1 2 3 4 5 6 7 8 9 10

If money were no object and you could do anything that you wanted, what would the perfect <u>home</u> environment look like, sound like, and feel like?

_____

_____

_____

_____

What is it in your home environment that is not satisfactory?

_____

_____

_____

_____

What is the challenge in your home environment?

_____

_____

_____

_____

What is missing in your home environment?

_____
_____
_____
_____

What stops this from happening?

_____
_____
_____
_____

What is your goal in this area?

_____
_____
_____
_____

For the above home environment goal, fill out a successful home environment S.M.A.R.T. Goal.

**Home environment S.M.A.R.T. goals (Meyer, 2019)**

**What is the Goal?** (Written in the future tense as if already achieved)

_____

_____

_____

**S - Specific.**

What will the goal accomplish?

_____

_____

_____

How and why will it be accomplished?

_____

_____

_____

**M - Measurable.**

How will you measure whether or not the goal has been reached (list at least two indicators)?

_____

_____

_____

**A - Achievable.**

Is it possible?

_____

_____

_____

Have others done it successfully?

_____

_____

_____

Do you have the necessary knowledge, skills, abilities, and resources to accomplish the goal?

_____

_____

_____

Will meeting the goal challenge you without defeating you?

_____

_____

_____

**R - Results-focused.**

What is the reason, purpose, or benefit of accomplishing the goal?

_____

_____

What is the outcome result (not the activities leading up to the result) of the goal?

_____

_____

_____

**T - Time-based.**

What is the established completion date and does that completion date create a practical sense of urgency?

_____

_____

_____

Revised Goal:

_____

_____

_____

_____

_____

**How do you want your WORK environment to feel?**

How would you rank your work environments below? Negative, neutral or positive experience and circle a number on the scale.

-10 -9 -8 -7 -6 -5 -4 -3 -2 -1 0 1 2 3 4 5 6 7 8 9 10

### Work Environment

If money were no object and you could do anything that you wanted, what would the perfect work environment look like, sound like and feel like?

_____
_____
_____
_____
_____

What is it in your work environment that is not satisfactory?

_____
_____
_____
_____

What is the challenge in your work environment?

_____
_____
_____
_____

What is missing in your work environment?

_____
_____
_____
_____
_____

What stops this from happening?

_____
_____
_____
_____
_____

What is your work goal in this area?

_____
_____
_____
_____
_____

From the above work environment goal fill out a successful work environment S.M.A.R.T. goal.

## Work Environment S.M.A.R.T Goal (Meyer, 2019)

**What is the Goal?** (Written in the future tense as if already achieved)

_____

_____

_____

### S - Specific.

What will the goal accomplish?

_____

_____

_____

How and why will it be accomplished?

_____

_____

_____

### M - Measurable.

How will you measure whether or not the goal has been reached (list at least two indicators)?

_____

_____

_____

**A - Achievable.**

Is it possible?

_____

_____

Have others done it successfully?

_____

_____

Do you have the necessary knowledge, skills, abilities, and resources to accomplish the goal?

_____

_____

Will meeting the goal challenge you without defeating you?

_____

_____

**R - Results-focused.**

What is the reason, purpose, or benefit of accomplishing the goal?

_____

_____

What is the outcome result (not the activities leading up to the result) of the goal?

**T - Time-based.**

What is the established completion date and does that completion date create a practical sense of urgency?

Revised Goal:

Notes:

## DIVORCE PARTY

# Chapter 9
## Career

"80% Of Life Is Just Showing Up" - *Woody Allen*

"Hard work beats talent every time."

"Do the work others aren't willing to do and you will get the things that others will never have."

"You can have everything in life you want, if you will just help other people get what they want." - *Zig Ziglar*

**What you will get in this chapter**

✓ The right attitude – G.Y.S.T.

– Get Your Sh!t Together

✓ Keeping your mind in a positive state

✓ 80% of life is just showing up

✓ Let it go and ways to release stress

✓ Visualization

✓ Breathing Exercises

✓ Mindfulness

✓ The 60 second Meditation

✓ E.F.T. Tapping or Emotional Freedom Technique

✓ Journaling

✓ Smiling and Laughing

✓ Acknowledge what is working

✓ What is your career passion?

✓ Where are the challenges and obstacles?

✓ Career W.F.O. Well-formed Outcome

### The right attitude – G.Y.S.T. Get Your Sh!t Together

Heads up, I am going to give you some tough love here. All feelings are valid. And if not managed, your feelings could affect your employment. It's time to kick yourself in the ass and get your shit together. Become proactive on your behalf and take action. If you are losing it at work emotionally; anger, sadness, or forgetfulness, not being productive, be proactive about it. Talk with you supervisor, HR, union business agent, and find out what work program through HR or the federal government laws give legal assurance for emotional and mental health support. Contact your physician, find a counselor, talk with a minister, or close friend.

It is totally normal, expected, and understandable for things to be emotionally difficult when experiencing divorce, loss, grieving, etc., and you have to take some action and enroll in the programs that will protect your employment and assist you with feeling better and being productive. Talk about what you are going through and take action with the available programs. Find out all the available resources to protect your career and have the attitude to persevere through this challenging time.

### Keeping your mind in a positive state

It's easy for me to say "hey turn that frown upside down" and it might not seem that easy at first or even piss you off. When you become aware of what you want instead, it gets easier to feel good anytime you want. When we are not thinking positively, it is that we are focused on something that is not positive. When you have awareness that our state is not working, we then have an opportunity to shift it to something that is working. This is critical because if we are not aware of it, we are running patterns unconsciously without conscious awareness. It is our choice to continue feeling like shit or choose "How do you want to feel instead?"

Negative emotions absolutely have a purpose and there is a distinct and appropriate time and place for them. And there are times they get in the way of our success. We want to build awareness of what triggers the negative state or be aware of our sensitive buttons being pushed. Then we can be consciously aware of the available resources and choices we can make when we are in those states so we can influence the best outcome for us and others.

Something triggered us and then we felt that negative feeling. A button gets pushed or a memory pops into our head and again we feel negative emotions. A feeling that we let happen and not resist only lasts about 90 seconds and it vanishes unless we choose to hold on to it and breathe life into it. Neurologically it begins to grow and take on a life of its own. Like a virus it grows, and it gets stronger if we let it.

We are either in one of two states in our life. We are either in a state of cause or effect. If we let a feeling affect us and our choices, we are a being at the effect of someone else, being a victim and giving our power to someone else to control us. We can also choose to empower ourselves. No matter what anyone in the world chooses to do to us, we don't control that, but we do choose how we respond and that empowers us. That is being in a state of at cause in our life.

**"The one thing you can't take away from me is the way I choose to respond to what you do to me. The last of one's freedoms is to choose one's attitude in any given circumstance."**

*- Viktor E. Frankl (Author of Man's Search for Meaning and Holocaust survivor)* (Frankl, 1959)

"Between stimulus and response there is a space. In that space is our power to choose our response. In our response lies our growth and our freedom"

— *Viktor E. Frankl* (Frankl, 1959)

Choose to allow that feeling to just be in the moment and allow that feeling that showed up to just be there for a moment. Breathe in deeply and let it out twice as slow, paying attention to your breath. Realize that we control our choices, and we do not control others choices

What is the feeling that you are challenged with getting out of easily? How do you want to feel instead? Think of a time in the past that you felt that desired feeling. Look through your eyes and what do you see, hear, and feel? Now, how do you feel differently?

We can create a shift from a non-positive state, feeling, or emotion into a positive state at any time and in any moment. But you have to play full out in this process with absolute conviction. That saying about "turn a negative into a positive" speaks to this.

First step is to awaken to conscious awareness of a desired state, what we want instead of what presently have. Then in our mind go back to a time we incredibly felt that way, and experience that state fully. What do you see, hear, and feel? Now double that feeling. Come back to now and how do you feel differently?

Our minds cannot distinguish between what is real and what is imagined. We literally are playing a past recording of a desirable state and that state will physiologically integrate into your body and mind.

Chemical reactions and hormone release enable that "feel good mood" to happen. The imagined becomes physiologically and mindfully real.

Practice these states and get really good at recalling them. Like a muscle you get out of this what you put into this and use it and you will retain it. Change your body position to a good feeling, move your eyes to a different location of focus, lift your head and look up to the left and then up to the right seeing yourself and how you desire to feel now. Exaggerate that feeling good state, turn up the volume, amplify that good feeling, alter the memory, and maximize the state. What are some positive states that you would benefit from? Happiness, laughing, feeling cared for, feeling important, powerful, energetic, peaceful? Write down some powerful states that you value and the memory of fully experiencing that powerful state.

Happiness

_____

_____

_____

Peaceful

_____

_____

_____

_____

# DIVORCE PARTY

Funny

_____

_____

_____

_____

Feeling Love

_____

_____

_____

_____

Empowered

_____

_____

_____

_____

Connected

_____

_____

_____

_____

Excitement

_____

___

___

___

Forgiving

___

___

___

Joyful

___

___

___

Caring

___

___

___

Appreciative

___

___

## "80% Of Life Is Just Showing Up" Woody Allen

Just show up. If you are reading this chapter, either your evaluation pointed you here, and you want to work on this, or you are committed to reading the entire book or just like to read. Regardless, I am glad you showed up! Finances are important to be able to pursue happiness and maintaining a career is the vehicle to get you there.

I do not want to suggest that you only have to show up to work but do not have to do work or that you can do half ass work. Most employers will be empathetic, but you do not want to wear out your welcome if it is the main theme you project. No matter how we feel you want to be as productive as possible at work. Give it all you got. Your commitment to persevere and maintain a good attitude despite what is going on will be appreciated by your employer. If you need professional help with your emotions reach out to those resources as soon as possible.

Eighty percent is just showing up is more about you can't do **anything** if you do not show up. Interestingly when we show up to work or the gym, we realize that there is a relief of pressure and a peace that overcomes us. Even though we didn't **feel** like we wanted to go and now that we are at work or at the gym, we might as well be productive. I have had some of my best workdays and workouts on days I didn't want to go and didn't want to show up.

The feeling of not wanting to go will pass when you get there. Build endurance that you know the feeling will pass with a little bit of time and when you get there. See, hear and feel what you look forward to with work. I tell myself on challenging days, "They pay me ridiculously well." When I think about the things I am able to do for myself and my kids because of work and the work benefits, I am pulled toward appreciating work.

It takes practice to build the automatic association and with practice it becomes automatic behavior to shift your state to appreciate the value of showing up. There is a bigger purpose that work is a part of that you absolutely value.

During your divorce party, even if you think you haven't changed, your workers will absolutely know you are experiencing stress. Usually they will give you the benefit of the doubt. However, if you don't maintain your relationships and work ethic, you could find yourself unemployed.

The chapter on relationships is connected to your career, supervisor, and co-workers. The maintenance of relationships is ongoing and some extra care and consideration is worth the effort when you are not having your best day. Knowing how to re-establish and build rapport is a highly valuable social skill and tool you can easily learn, and worth looking at in the relationship chapter.

Eighty percent of life is just showing up. I did not believe it until I witnessed just how far an employee could go and keep their job. This is a rare exception but a real story that I witnessed. Again I don't want to minimize the value of your productivity on the job, how hard you work, and being excellent at work. I do want to share a story with you that taught me the extreme meaning of this quote and I have been amazed witnessing it several times with different people and genders.

# DIVORCE PARTY

Years ago, I was learned about a fellow employee who frequently showed up to work hungover or still drunk from an all-night to morning of partying. His life was falling apart in front of us.

Alcohol, drugs, DUI's, arrests, falling out of a car after a night of partying and going straight to work after. He had lost his license so someone had to drive him to work. His driver told a story about picking him up one morning as he rolled out of someone else's car, literally just getting home as he was being picked up for work. Beer cans falling out of the car as he rolled out and onto the ground. The dude was definitely entertaining, yet sadly, a mess getting messier. It was interesting to get updates on his latest adventures, near misses, and tragedies of his life style.

During my divorce I was far from perfect and felt additional pressure at work. I had my own demons that I was dealing with, trying to maintain my life, and keep my emotions and anger in control. I had challenges focusing and completing work. I felt there was increased pressure to work faster. I would just finish one job and then run to the next. Again, faster, faster, faster. I thought I was working as fast as I could but I know that my concentration suffered. Maybe I was reading more into it than what was really there.

In my own frustration, I began to question, compare, and judge the employee that was a train wreck. How is it that he had not lost his job yet? A simple drug test would have done him in immediately. He did, in fact, show up. Not perfect, not sober, not drug free, not without drama, not without an incredible fanfare and display of WTF, but he did, in fact, show up.

I am not condoning or encouraging the dangerous behavior or lifestyle. I am saying show the fu%k up. No matter how difficult it is, or how your own self-doubt and negative self-talk may discourage you to take a day off or call in sick, just show up and do your very best. That is all we can do. Show up to do the work and do your very best. Show up for your employer and do your very best. Show up for your kids and do your very best. Show up for yourself and do your very best.

Okay, I admittedly think that is probably the worst ever example of 80% of life is showing up but damn, they never fired the guy. The value in that lesson is I know how difficult it is to show up to work, going through depression, the emotional rollercoaster, the self-doubt and fear of losing your job, but if you do not show up, all your fears will possibly come true. Here is a little more positive example of how to apply this 80% rule.

Before I lost the 100 pounds, I started weight lifting in the mornings. I set some rules and a goal that I had to lift at least one weight and if I didn't feel like working out, I wouldn't. Fascinating thing was, I discovered that I always worked out past the one weight. By setting easy goals you can absolutely achieve, you will actually push yourself farther, and you are always successful. My easily achievable goal was to just show up and lift one weight. In that whole experience there was only 1 day when I had gotten pretty sick that I showed up, lifted one weight and said, "Not today." I didn't beat myself up because I did achieve the daily goal of just showing up and lifting 1 weight. I also recognized that just showing up had created a powerful habit and propelled me to be consistent.

That's my take on the 80% is just showing up quote and consider how it applies to work. Just showing up is critical, in fact, without showing up, you are not even given the opportunity to do the other 20%. Even if you don't feel like it with work, know that it will turn into feeling like you want to stay, now that you are there. In fact, you will realize it was not as bad as it felt like it would be and you are actually glad that you made it.

Set goals that are easy enough, that you absolutely are guaranteed you will achieve them. I will take a shower, I will get my clothes on, I will drive to work, I will trust that I will be thankful I showed up. Where attention goes the energy flows. Just show up.

**Let it go and ways to release stress**

Would it be of value to you to let go of stress? Let's talk about relaxing. Excellent ways include breathing exercises, mindfulness, meditation, visualization, E.F.T. Tapping or Emotional Freedom Technique, exercising, yoga, journaling, smiling, laughing, focusing on a positive purpose, volunteering, and contributing by giving unconditional love to others.

**Letting go of stress exercise**

Stress, how do you know when you are doing it?

_____

_____

_____

Where do you feel it in your body? Move it outside of your body. How does it feel different now?

_____

_____

_____

_____

Does it have a color? Change the color or intensity. How does it look different now?

_____

_____

_____

_____

Does it have a sound? Decrease it or change it to a way that is soothing. How does it sound different now?

_____

_____

_____

_____

Does it have a rotation? Grab a hold of it and reverse the direction. Spin it faster and faster, double that speed and then double it again. How does it feel different now?

_____

_____

_____

_____

### Breathing Exercises

Breathing exercises are easy and highly effective with releasing stress by activating the parasympathetic nervous system, slowing down your heart rate and decreasing your blood pressure. You can do these exercises anywhere.

Breathe in slowly through your nose and out through your mouth. Breathe in deeply, fully extending your belly out and holding it. Release and breathe out twice as slow. Breathe in, nourishing your body and mind with fresh oxygen, then exhaling out twice as slow, releasing all that energy you were holding onto. Continue breathing like this and repeat to a count of ten times. Now, notice and write down how you feel different.

_____

_____

_____

_____

### Mindfulness

Intentionally bringing one's attention to what is occurring in the present moment without judging is mindfulness. There are infinite ways to experience it and exercise it. Find what works for you.

**Simple mindfulness exercises.**

- Close your eyes and listen to a sound for 60 seconds
- Stroke your hands for 60 seconds.
- Mindful breathing for 60 seconds
- Stretch your body for 60 seconds
- Think about what you appreciate about today for 60 seconds
- Pick an object and notice its details for 60 seconds
- Move your awareness to your feet, your elbow, your breath, your ears, your left thumb, your nostrils, your right toe, what sounds do you hear, what is the temperature, how do your clothes feel, what colors are vibrant, what do you notice least of all, what do you appreciate?

**The 60 second Meditation**

There are many forms of meditation and we're going to make it easy and simple to use anywhere. Quick and easy, piece of cake! This is the 60 second meditation. One purpose of meditation is to release all analyzing and thinking and instead, think about not thinking about much of anything at all.

- Take a deep breath in through your nose as you count to 20.
- Hold that breath in for 20 seconds.
- Let that breath out your mouth slowly counting to 20. Practice until you can do it. You may have to start with a 30 second meditation. Counting 10 - 10-10.

## E.F.T. Tapping or Emotional Freedom Technique

E.F.T. is a powerful and highly effective state changing tool that is easy to do anywhere. It works exceptionally well with anxiety, calming the mind and body. It is based upon the acupuncture or acupressure points in the body known as 'meridians.' Look it up on the internet and you will find unlimited free resources and how-to videos.

Notes:

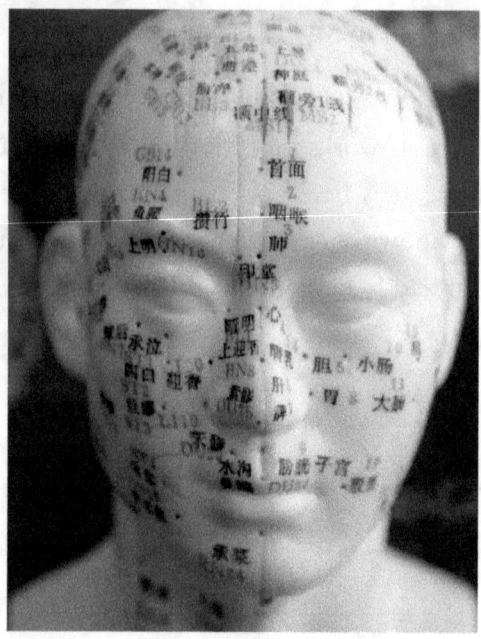

## Journaling

An excellent way to feel calmer and more in control is to write it down on paper or in a phone notepad. Something magical happens, something releases just by writing down your thoughts and fully expressing yourself on paper. Allow yourself to fully release the feelings that you have been holding onto inside. Let them go without judgment or concern. Journaling will give insight you didn't know was already there. Just let your hand flow and allow it all out, whatever shows up. Write your thought down now, let the pen flow freely and without judgement whatever is on your mind right now ...

_____

_____

_____

## DIVORCE PARTY

_____

_____

_____

_____

_____

_____

_____

_____

**Smiling and Laughing**

Feel like a bad parent? FACT - The Australian Quokka, toss their babies at predators so they can escape. Now that is just beautifully funny and an option if they don't behave. Practice not smiling. It takes more muscles to frown than it does to smile. Isn't that silly? You actually burn more calories to not smile than it takes to smile, and how easy it is too smile. It is more work and effort not to smile. In fact, I don't want you to smile. Think about a time that you were so happy that it hurt to smile and don't try to smile. The muscles in your face hurt so good but don't smile yet! And if you want to smile now, you can easily. Try it on if you are not already smiling. Think of someone that makes you smile and smile even more. If you are not smiling yet, for the love of God put a freaking smile on that face. Force that smile and those muscles to smile until you have tears in your eyes. Did you know that it is scientifically not possible to smile and not feel happy at the same time? It is not possible for those two things to exist at the same time. Isn't that interesting? Practice not smiling.

Finding humor and laughter on the other hand, is easy to do. Laughing, like smiling, drops feel good dopamine into the pleasure center of your mind. Like smiling, you can take on the physiology of laughing and you begin to feel better. There is even laughing meditation groups that sit around and practice laughing.

There are many other ways to get that addictive feel good dopamine drop that laughing brings. Rent movies that are funny or in the comedy genre. Also available are famous comedians who have exclusive specials featuring them. Pandora and other radio services have comedy channels. Locally, there are comedy and improv shows, many offer classes, lessons, and the opportunity to do stand-up at an open mic night or perform. Performing is healing! There are plays and musicals that have funny content. Practice laughing in front of your mirror while naked, and seriously that is funny. Get out and laugh and feel good like James Brown! Hayyyyyyyyyyyyyyyy! I feel good! Nananananananana!

**Acknowledge what is working**

We can be such assholes to ourselves. We focus on what's wrong with us and we shy away from or shun acknowledging that we are really good at some things. It is probably that we are raised with some limiting beliefs about "you should not brag about yourself" or "don't be self-centered" or maybe even a guilt belief that "I feel guilty about feeling good about myself" or "others will hate me or be jealous of my success or happiness and shun me".

If you are narcissistic you probably are not reading this book. So, what is wrong with loving and acknowledging ourselves? We should remind ourselves that we are successful in many areas and with many things despite the fact that we are human and not perfect. Write down what is already working with your career and what skills and capabilities do you have that are worth celebrating?

_____

_____

_____

_____

**What is your career passion?**

What did you want to become when you grew up and are you doing that now? Probably not. Of course, our realities are different between then and now. However, I will assert that when you were younger, you knew what you wanted and demanded it. You knew what you were passionate about and went after it. How are you now expressing or not expressing your passion now?

_____

_____

_____

_____

If money and time were not an object, what would you want to be doing that inspires you, fulfills your purpose, excites and ignites you, even if you were not getting paid to do it?

_____

_____

_____

_____

_____

When have you felt the most alive in your life? What were you doing? How did it feel?

_____

_____

_____

_____

_____

What is a career passion goal of yours?

_____

_____

_____

_____

_____

**Where are the challenges and obstacles?**

Sometimes we have to take a realistic snapshot of our career and this is what we call the truth. Look at this as an opportunity for self-development, growth, and building your value of employment. Showing your employer that you are motivated to improve, add value to your career, and take action toward it, will speak louder than anything you can say. Actions speak louder than words.

Evaluate your career. Enroll your supervisor or those close to you and ask for some honest feedback. Look at your career and without judgment ask yourself what areas, skills, and capabilities, behaviors, or beliefs, can you improve that will have the biggest impact on boosting your value at work?

_____

_____

_____

_____

_____

Complete a W.F.O. – Well-Formed Outcome for your career.

**Career W.F.O.**

**- Well-Formed Outcome (Meyer, 2019)**

1. With your career, (stated in the positive, what you want, not what you don't want.) What do you want?

_____

# DIVORCE PARTY

_____

_____

_____

_____

Can it be initiated by you?

_____

_____

_____

_____

Can it be controlled by you?

_____

_____

_____

_____

Is it a large outcome or is it of manageable chunk size? Chunk down into smaller outcomes if necessary.

_____

_____

_____

2. How will you know when you have got it? (what will your evidence be? Describe in sensory terms, what will you see, what will you hear, what will you feel?)

_____

_____

_____

_____

3. Where, when, and with whom do you want it? (What is the context)

_____

_____

_____

_____

Under what circumstances do you want it?

_____

_____

_____

_____

4. Other considerations for the outcome: What are the positive and negative consequences of getting your outcome?

What resources do you need to get your outcome? (Information, Information, attitude, internal state, training, money, help or support from others, etc.)

What are you already doing to already achieve your outcome?

What will having that outcome achieve for you? (Determine the intention beyond the specific outcome.)

_____
_____
_____
_____

Is the first step to achieving your outcome specific and achievable?

_____
_____
_____
_____

Is there more than one way to get your outcome?

_____
_____
_____
_____

What time frames are involved?

_____
_____

What stops you from having your outcome now?

5. Imagine stepping into the future having fully achieved your outcome. Look back and determine what steps were required to achieve the outcome now that you have it. (write them down)

Notes:

# Chapter 10
## Fun and Recreation

"All work and no play, makes Jack a dull boy" - James Howell

"Everyone deserves happiness"

Create in me a pure heart, O God, and renew a steadfast spirit within me. Do not cast me from your presence or take your Holy Spirit from me. Restore to me the joy of your salvation and grant me a willing spirit, to sustain me. - Psalm 51:10-12

**What you will get in this chapter**

- ✓ Why you need FUN in your life
- ✓ What do you love to do for fun?
- ✓ Recharge your batteries, and keep going and going
- ✓ Wake up from unconsciousness
- ✓ Join a group a local group
- ✓ Find groups you are looking for online
- ✓ Can't find what you are looking for – start a club
- ✓ Get serious about laughing, it will make you smile
- ✓ 35 Frugal Activities to do and Stay-cations
- ✓ Fun & Recreation S.M.A.R.T. goal

**Why you need FUN in your life**

Is there no fun in your life? What happened? There was a time we couldn't wait to wake up or couldn't even go to sleep, in anticipation of yet another incredible fun day full of adventure, games, pretend, imagination, bologna and cheese sandwiches, cartoons, Gilligan's Island, and endless chocolate milk!

"Where have all the good times gone?" - *Van Halen*

I remember one winter when I was child, the radio was on and announced that a horrible blizzard was coming. I erupted into cheers, joy, excitement, happiness, and yelling at the opportunity to get to play in the snow. My older, working brother was pissed. I asked him "why don't you like snow?" ... And now I know! I usually have the same answer he had, because of what snow brings if you focus on work and not fun.

I have lived in Illinois my entire life. A coworker was talking about when he lived in Michigan. At that time, I personally hated winters. I had to ask, "How did you do it?" He said, "Do what?" I inquired further, "How did you live in Michigan, aren't the winters like, terrible there?" He replied, "We actually loved winters and looked forward to them!"

I was shocked "WHAT??? You looked forward to what?" He replied, "There was so much to do in the Winter and we hated to see it go. There was snowmobiling, ice fishing, skiing, hockey season, ice skating, really fun snowmobile weekends and trails at the cabin, we had a couple friends and would go bar hopping by snowmobile."

I couldn't believe his joy as he lit up with excitement remembering his time there. It seemed ridiculous to me. I could not have imagined anyone looking forward to something like that ... something I didn't like; snow and cold. Yet he focused on what they could do, and they were happy about it. They had fun and anticipated its arrival. The purpose of fun and recreation is to recharge your batteries and create a forward motivation and drive. A powerful want to work hard, so we can play hard.

Some key take-aways that I learned from him.

1. What we focus on expands. Why not focus on what you want instead of what you do not want?

2. Have something to look forward to.

Do not focus on someone else's happiness. Focus on your own, what makes you happy. Some people like asparagus and some people do not. Some people love tomatoes and some do not. If he was to focus on all the reasons that I didn't like winter, he potentially could expand his own attitude and focus on my negatives.

**Have something to look forward to**

There is something magical that happens when we have something to look forward to. This creates a positive anticipation. Have you ever gone to bed so excited about something incredible that was happening the next day that you could not easily sleep?

Going back to what we talked about with N.L.P. and future pacing. If we have nothing in the future to look forward to then where is our focus? Either in the moment of now or the past. Depending on your past you will focus on positive or negative things depending upon triggers you experience that will replay the video in your mind of those moments. If your focus is on the present moment then how that feels depends upon your present state.

By throwing things into the future we create a magnetic pull toward the future and a positive focus on what is to come. But we must take action. It is something we have to intentionally do. It's not going to happen on its own. Even just planning a weekly cup of coffee with a friend will create something to look forward to and something to have to do and something to take your mind off of everything else. What is something that you have enjoyed doing in the past and can do again in the future?

_____

_____

Set your intention right now to schedule that in the future and put it on the calendar. What is the date, what are you doing and with whom?

_____

_____

When I was going through my divorce and I enrolled in the David Ramsey Financial Peace University class I was so happy to have something to do and look forward to for the next 2 months. When I started the various groups, clubs, and organizations I not only looked forward to the events, but I experienced and continue to have several friend relationships that started with those groups.

When I found the Divorce Care program I so looked forward to that weekly class. I expressed with the instructor of that class that I was feeling lonely. He said to me that when he went through his divorce he decided to meet with a fellow friend that was in his divorce care program weekly for a cup of coffee. He said that he grew to look forward to that weekly meeting with his friend and encouraged me to do the same. Not for therapy conversation but just to have something to look forward to and take my mind off of feeling alone. He said that he still meets with his friend weekly.

**What do you love to do for fun?**

What do you love to do for fun, recreation, rest, and relaxation now?

_____

What were some of the most fun, enjoyable, and pleasurable moments looking back on your life?

**Recharge your batteries, - and keep going and going**

Think back to an incredible vacation. How did that feel? How did it feel going back to work? Think back to a walk in the woods. How did that feel as you experienced the journey? Have you ever left 10" of snow at the airport and were magically transported to another sunnier location with 86 degrees and sunny blue skies? How did that feel?

I remember a wonderful vacation with my family where we went to an amusement park when the kids were young. I am a morning person and use to getting up 4 A.M. – 5 A.M. I remember getting up early and sneaking out, not to wake anyone, to get some continental coffee by myself.

I was use to rushing around in the morning. It took some time for me to relax and breathe deep, adjusting to the realization I had nowhere to go and no one was expecting my arrival. It was wonderful. I found myself just thinking freely. How enjoyable this peace felt. How we really, really, really, should do this more often! I began to notice something else emerging. An excitement. A part of myself who wanted more for my family. Creativity began to flow as I thought about ideas and ways to create opportunities and additional income to do the vacations more.

It was like this voice in me, that I had been too busy to hear, and too busy to feel that desire and passion within me. It was exciting. It filled me with energy and I didn't want the voice to go away.

Have you experienced anything similar? It's like we get so wrapped up into the drift of everyday life. Like when we arrive at a location and not remembering the drive or landmarks we passed. Unconscious auto pilot. Alarm goes off and it starts all over again without much of anything changing day to day.

### Wake up from unconsciousness

Doing something different will force you into consciousness. Vacations do this. And that feeling of aliveness that comes from vacationing can be experienced in other ways. You have patterns of behavior you learn to the point of unconsciousness. Consciously rebel against the comfortable and known. Drive home a different route. Brush your teeth with the opposite hand. Cross your arms and then reverse your top hand to the bottom. Use the opposite hand while eating.

By consciously doing new behavior you are creating new neurological pathways and connections. Get comfortable with trying new things and being uncomfortable. Take notice of how purposefully being uncomfortable feels. Do something new. Listen to a new piece of music. Learn a new language, skill, capability, take a class. Take a walk on a trail and reverse the direction. There is infinite newness and aliveness to explore. When you catch yourself doing something by habit, change it, make it new. Take the cliché' and transform it into something new! Wake up! Notice how you feel differently!

**Join a local group**

There are so many awesome opportunities in your community as well as the online communities. Joining an established club or group has many benefits. You can learn something new. You can form social bonds. You can also volunteer and contribute your skills and capabilities to add to others' lives. There are lots of things you can find and do locally. Locally there are organizations like:

- Chamber of Commerce – resource for opportunities, clubs, organizations, volunteer opportunities

- Toastmasters International – learn public speaking

- The library

- Clubs – photography, chess, astronomy, swimming, walking and running

- Y.M.C.A.

- Churches

- City Recreation League

- Park District

- David Ramsey Financial Peace University
- Divorce Care – support group

**Find groups you are looking for online**

Online there are so many opportunities! Even if you can't find something locally that is appealing to you, the internet brings the entire world to you. Some cool places to find people, clubs, organizations, hobbies, and interests as well as places to learn new things.

- Meetup.com – my favorite! Anything you can imagine, hobbies, interests, support groups and most are free!
- Facebook, Twitter, Instagram, Snapchat, Tumblr, Google, groups.
- Udemy – learn something new!
- Google search – anything, include city and state to find clubs and organizations near you or online.

**Can't find what you are looking for**

**– Start a club**

I consider myself an introvert, but I really blossomed with creating my own clubs, meetups, and organizations online and in person. All out of necessity. I wanted to learn photography. The closest camera club was an hour and forty-five minutes away which I gladly drove, until I learned enough about photography to start a local club. I initiated and formed; ".raw Adventure camera club" through Meetup. I hosted outings, classes, and get-togethers for about 3 years.

Meetup is a really cool community for just about anything you are interested in doing. Pretty much anything you can imagine is there. You might have to travel but you can get connected with some really awesome people doing the things you love. If you start a group there are tons of people already on meetup that are probably looking for a group like yours.

I ran into several volunteer opportunities with the camera club and one that was special to my heart was for an event called "Help Portrait." A wonderful giving event for the less fortunate.

The organization is all volunteer and local events spring up around Thanksgiving and Christmas. Everything from volunteer hair and makeup, photographers, DJ music, donated food, drinks and clothing items for colder months. From shelters to homeless to prisoners, people get made up with haircuts, make up, donated suits and clothing, and get a free professional portrait photo shoot and get free photos they get to have and share with family and friends. It is a beautiful community event.

After volunteering and building my confidence with the event and my photography skills, I decided to host 3 Help Portrait events in my hometown and neighboring town. I was amazed how many volunteers freely gave over their time and skills. It was a wonderful community during a challenging time during my divorce. Little did those that received their photographs, food, winter clothing, and beauty care were giving far more to us all.

I went on to form a local N.L.P. And hypnosis meetup group, a marathon training group, a walking club, started a local Toastmasters International group, host photography classes online, web site design, coaching, a popular and successful singles group where we would do fun activities, dinner, bowling, and comedy club outings. It really helped me through some lonely feeling times, and many others in the same boat experiencing the same thing.

You don't have to be the expert to start a club or meetup and become the group leader. Be willing to be open and honest that you don't have all the answers but willing to find them. The line to become a leader is almost nonexistent and others are waiting and looking for someone to step up into leadership. If you can't find what you are looking for, create it. You absolutely can do it. You have my permission! My negative self-talk was screaming when I considered starting a group. But seriously, what is stopping you? There may not be anyone else who will start the group if you don't start it! Just do it!

**Get serious about laughing, it will make you smile!**

Laughter is healing. Part of being in my family has always been humor. I am sure it has its roots originating as a coping mechanism for survival in my family. I had a challenging childhood growing up as did many children of divorce and separation. My parents separated when I was about four or five-years-old. Humor was my escape. Humor, being funny, and getting laughs made friends. Humor could save you from getting your ass kicked if you could make them laugh. Humor felt good.

I remember the early Saturday Night Live cast starting in 1975 and the crazy skits of comedy. I couldn't wait to watch the late night S.N.L. And there was a lonely, hauntingly sad feeling listening to the ending saxophone and the announcer Don Pardo signing off. Back then they didn't have the 24-hour stations like they do today. The S.N.L. Show was my highlight for the weekend.

I didn't realize how significant humor was for my family until my senior year and the death of my father. At the funeral, yes, of course we were sad that we had lost our dad. And we were also making some people feel uncomfortable. Some having jaw dropping expressions from our coping and dark sense of humor. I actually felt bad, that maybe I should have felt sadder. I hadn't practiced or trained for how I should have felt. For my family it was appropriate.

There have been countless studies on how laughing and smiling is medically therapeutic and can even heal your mind, body, and spirit. There is no absolute conclusive evidence that laughter can cure cancer or other diseases, but several have made this claim.

Norman Cousins (Cousins, 1979) in the 1970's was a successful writer and editor-in-chief for the Saturday Review. He was hospitalized with a crippling disease. Norman checked himself into the hotel across the street from the hospital and constantly exposed himself to funny and humorous films of the Marx Brothers and Candid Camera. He read a variety of funny books. He discovered that if he experienced a good 10 minutes of belly laughter, he could sleep pain free for 20 minutes. Little by little he improved and was famously known as the man who laughed himself back to health.

Laughter therapy is used with patients to reduce stress, pain, create relaxation, enhance the quality of life, and boost the immune system.

Laughing is more fun than crying! During my divorce I sought out comedy clubs, improv clubs, open mic night, rented comedies and co-median videos, listened to audiobooks on iTunes of comedians including Bob Newhart and Steve Martin, and listened to comedy radio channels on satellite radio.

The laughing felt incredibly good and connected me with people. I made new friends. The laughing gave me something positive to focus on and distract my mind from everything else that was out of my control. And like a muscle, my mind would grow stronger from the laughter exposure. I would find myself looking for the punch line in the tragedy of divorce and life.

What are some ways you can intentionally laugh and who can you enroll to join you? What comedy source has worked in the past that painfully had you laughing? What are some things you want to do for some laughter therapy?

_____

_____

_____

_____

**35 Frugal Activities to do and *Stay-cations***

1) Enjoy nature

2) Have a picnic

3) Tour factories

4) Visit the library

5) Try a new recipe

6) Frisbee golf

7) Go hiking on trails

8) Visit local festivals

9) Community service or clean-up projects

10) Go camping

11) Play a board or card game

12) Geocaching

13) Go to pick your own – farms

14) See a ball game

15) Go to the fair

16) Go fishing

17) Take a boat ride

18) Farmers Market

19) Visit or contact an old friend

20) Sign up for community activities or classes

21) Host a book club

22) Go dancing

23) Take an exercise class

24) Build something

25) Play lawn games

26) Spend time with the kids

27) Host a movie night

28) Play miniature or regular golf

29) Go to a museum

30) Go to an amusement park

31) Create an obstacle course

32) Go bowling

33) Outdoor concert

34) Host a barbecue

35) Go for a bike ride

What are some fun ideas that you have thought about in this chapter that you want to do in the future?

_____

_____

_____

_____

**Fun & Recreation**

- S.M.A.R.T. goal (Meyer, 2019)

What would you like to create/ What is a goal you want to accomplish with fun and recreation? Fill out a smart goal below and have some fun!

**What is the Goal?** (Written in the future tense as if already achieved)

_____

**S - Specific.**

What will the goal accomplish?

How and why will it be accomplished?

**M - Measurable.**

How will you measure whether or not the goal has been reached (list at least two indicators)?

**A - Achievable.**

Is it possible?

Have others done it successfully?

_____

_____

_____

Do you have the necessary knowledge, skills, abilities, and resources to accomplish the goal?

_____

_____

_____

Will meeting the goal challenge you without defeating you?

_____

_____

_____

**R - Results-focused.**

What is the reason, purpose, or benefit of accomplishing the goal?

_____

_____

_____

What is the outcome result (not the activities leading up to the result) of the goal?

_____

_____

**T - Time-based.**

What is the established completion date and does that completion date create a practical sense of urgency?

_____

_____

_____

Revised Goal:

_____

_____

_____

_____

_____

Notes:

_____

_____

_____

_____

_____

_____

# DIVORCE PARTY

# Conclusion

You have traveled so far in this book and congratulations for your commitment, growth and your successes you have experienced by being persistent and focusing on the positives!

"All good things must come to an end," as they say and here we are. And really this is just the beginning for you! There is this hero's journey that plays out again and again and again. From the beginning of time and forward throughout all time. Do you have time for one more fascinating story?

This book is always available for you to dive back into and find resources and support. As life happens and changes so will our challenges.

In conclusion we have covered why you first came here. We have discussed how this book works, how to triage your life and discover what is working and what areas have the most desired opportunity for change and growth. There are 8 key areas in everyone's life.

**The 8 Key Areas of Life**

1. Health
2. Spirituality
3. Finances
4. self-development
5. relationships
6. environment career
7. fun/recreation

Remember that circus clown and those spinning plates. It takes some upfront effort to cause the inertia to overcome the gravity. Once the plates are spinning it only takes a little maintenance to keep all the plates spinning. Get intentional about maintaining all the spinning plates.

- WHAT DO YOU WANT INSTEAD? Practice asking this over and over and over. Perhaps the most important question for us all to ask.

- We are not worth anything to anyone if we are not worth something to ourselves first.

-What is most important should never be sacrificed for what is least important.

- We must love ourselves first so we can love others. When we love ourselves, we can reflect it outward to others.

- We must forgive ourselves first so we can forgive others.

- Forgiveness is not for the other person forgiveness is for you.

- We must focus on what we want instead of what we don't want.

- We only control our choices.

- We empower our lives not by what happens to us, but what we choose to do next in response.

- What we focus on expands and when we focus in a positive way on any of the key areas of our life, that area of our life will heal, and move toward improvement and excellence.

- Remember to breathe on purpose.

The conclusion is also just the beginning for you and for me, and I am excited for you to move forward with your next hero's journey. Be well and I am sending out to you love, light, healing and the breath of life. Remember to take time to breathe and let it out twice as slow. Do this as often as you can.

Notes:

_____

_____

_____

_____

_____

_____

_____

# AFTERWARD

Wow. I can't believe I am writing the end of this book! Accomplishing a goal that started over 10 years ago. I felt that there was a lack of resources for someone going through a divorce. It's awkward and challenging for everyone. Several friends of mine that experienced a divorce about the same time as I did, commented that I should put something together to help others going through a divorce. Even just a simple book that had all the resources and books I read, and I reached out to get support. And that is what lead to this book.

I was assembling the book in a folder at first. Just notes and ideas I would have while driving. Everything from napkins to toilet paper anything to capture the ideas. I also would cut out magazine and newspaper articles. Later I would transcribe ideas to electronic documents and store them on my computer but still keeping the original pieces of paper.

As technology progressed, I discovered dragon Voice software and this created a speech to text electronic document. This was transformational for me as I am mainly an auditory learner and loved speaking about a story or article. I was able to start massing documents.

Last year my youngest daughter turned 21 and I felt that now was the time to get busy to make this book real. My utmost concern about writing this book was that I be caring of my children and my ex-wife's feelings and protecting them from anything that would unintentionally but possibly offensive or too much information. I have reached out to them all and requested their approval of this book and that I can edit it anytime.

I also include personal examples of my life that not everyone who knows me may know about me. Thing I am not particularly proud of or excited to share. It was more important for me to authentic, transparent and vulnerable about topics like addiction and suicide because if one person experiences it that is worth sharing with others who may be experiencing the same thing. If this book saves one life, it will all have been worth writing it.

I hired a book writing coach in 2018 and what seemed overwhelming began to turn into possible and real. I had declared that this be published by the end of the year in 2019. And the power of declaration is humbling. Here we are today 12-22-2019 3:23 p.m. in Danville, Illinois in the USA about to make that publishing happen.

All that is left to do is to share with 40 plus friends that have volunteered to read the pre-publishing edited version of Divorce Party in exchange for their feedback. I have one final professional editing and then it's publish time December 28th 2019.

I know. I know. I know. Everyone probably thinks they have some great ideas. Great enough to write a book? I truly believe this body of work in this book is transformational for anyone going through a divorce and willing to intentionally focus on the positive ideas, take action and do the work in the exercises. I have seen amazing, rapid healing and transformation with those having reoccurring emotional trauma and emotional states. Moving from a severe abreaction to an incredible positively changed emotional life and healing.

This is absolutely a unique book and nothing like it exists at the time of this writing that I could find. I believe it fills a need for those looking for a collective and specific resource all in one place. Unique that it covers all the key areas of everyone's lives and offers tools, exercises action steps to move toward what you want instead.

Moving forward, join us online at www.divorcekeys.com Sign up for the mailing list that occasionally sends out upcoming webinars, workshops, trainings and FREE offers. Join us in a workshop online or in person. If you are a coach or interested in helping others, we offer a coaching certification training covering coaching essentials and the fundamentals of divorce coaching using the methods covered in this book.

# Appendix A
## Quotes and Scripture

**Introduction**

"Achieve your goals, not for what they will give you, but for who you must become in order to achieve them." – Jim Rohn

**Chapter 1 – Putting the puzzle pieces back together**

"Things which matter most must never be at the mercy of things which matter least." - Johann Wolfgang von Goethe

**Chapter 2 – Wheel of Life**

"Too much of one thing can end up creating stress; this is something that no one needs in their life. But living a life in balance can provide harmony and peace." - Catherine Pulsifer, Birthday Wishes for a Best Friend

"What you vividly imagine, ardently desire, sincerely believe and enthusiastically act upon must inevitably come to pass. - Paul J. Meyer

"Too much sanity may be madness and maddest of all: to see life as it is, and not as it should be!" - The Man of La Mancha

**Chapter 3 - Spirituality**

"God speaks loudly in the moments between silence"

"I don't mind so much, a minister condemning my soul

to eternal hell, as long as he has tears of sadness in his eyes,

but not tears of joy"- Jim Rohn

"The atoms of our bodies are traceable to stars that manufactured them in their cores and exploded these enriched ingredients across our galaxy, billions of years ago. For this reason, we are biologically connected to every other living thing in the world. We are chemically connected to all molecules on Earth. And we are atomically connected to all atoms in the universe. We are not figuratively, but literally stardust." - Neil deGrasse Tyson

"No temptation has overtaken you except what is common to mankind. And God is faithful; he will not let you be tempted beyond what you can bear. But when you are tempted, he will also provide a way out so that you can endure it." - Corinthians 10-13

"Why do you look at the speck of sawdust in your brother's eye and pay no attention to the plank in your own eye? How can you say to your brother, 'Let me take the speck out of your eye,' when all the time there is a plank in your own eye? You hypocrite, first take the plank out of your own eye, and then you will see clearly to remove the speck from your brother's eye." - Mathew 7:3-5

"Resentment is like taking poison and waiting for the other person to die."- Malachy McCourt

**The Parable of the Lost Son** - 11 Jesus continued: "There was a man who had two sons. 12 The younger one said to his father, 'Father, give me my share of the estate.' So, he divided his property between them.

13 "Not long after that, the younger son got together all he had, set off for a distant country and there squandered his wealth in wild living. 14 After he had spent everything, there was a severe famine in that whole country, and he began to be in need. 15 So he went and hired himself

out to a citizen of that country, who sent him to his fields to feed pigs. 16 He longed to fill his stomach with the pods that the pigs were eating, but no one gave him anything.

17 "When he came to his senses, he said, 'How many of my father's hired servants have food to spare, and here I am starving to death! 18 I will set out and go back to my father and say to him: Father, I have sinned against heaven and against you. 19 I am no longer worthy to be called your son; make me like one of your hired servants.' 20 So he got up and went to his father.

"But while he was still a long way off, his father saw him and was filled with compassion for him; he ran to his son, threw his arms around him and kissed him.

21 "The son said to him, 'Father, I have sinned against heaven and against you. I am no longer worthy to be called your son.'

22 "But the father said to his servants, 'Quick! Bring the best robe and put it on him. Put a ring on his finger and sandals on his feet. 23 Bring the fattened calf and kill it. Let's have a feast and celebrate. 24 For this son of mine was dead and is alive again; he was lost and is found.' So, they began to celebrate.

25 "Meanwhile, the older son was in the field. When he came near the house, he heard music and dancing. 26 So he called one of the servants and asked him what was going on. 27 'Your brother has come,' he replied, 'and your father has killed the fattened calf because he has him back safe and sound.'

28 "The older brother became angry and refused to go in. So his father went out and pleaded with him. 29 But he answered his father,

'Look! All these years I've been slaving for you and never disobeyed your orders. Yet you never gave me even a young goat so I could celebrate with my friends. 30 But when this son of yours who has squandered your property with prostitutes comes home, you kill the fattened calf for him!'

31 "'My son,' the father said, 'you are always with me, and everything I have is yours. 32 But we had to celebrate and be glad, because this brother of yours was dead and is alive again; he was lost and is found.'" Luke 15:11-32 NIV

**The story of the frog and the scorpion** - One day a scorpion and a frog happen to meet on the bank of the river at the same time. The frog was about to jump in the river and swim to the other side, but before he jumps, the scorpion comes up to negotiate. The scorpion says: "Mr. Frog, it has always been my dream to get to the other side of the river and I am a scorpion and I can't swim. Would you be so generous to let me hop on your back, and you swim across the river and transport me to the other side so that I can fulfill my destiny?" The frog gets to thinking, and says: "No way! Scorpions sting frogs and kill them. I would get halfway out there where the water is too deep, you would sting me and I would drown. That's not going to happen today or any day my friend." The scorpion shook his head and said to the frog: "You're not thinking right with your tiny frog mind you were given. Think about it logically. If I stung you out there, yes you would die, but so would I! I'm not interested in committing suicide, I just want to get to the other side to finally see what life has to offer, maybe greener pastures. Please take me, it has always been my dream since I was a little scorpion," as a tear began to form in the scorpion's eye. And the frog says: "OK, OK, OK, that makes sense. Hop on on and we will get you to the other side." So, the frog turns around and the scorpion hops on the frog's back and the frog starts off across the river. The frog is swimming and sure enough half way across the scorpion stings the frog. The toxin begins to paralyze the frog and the frog is struggling to stay above water. Going down 2nd, 3rd, now 4th time, the frog can't believe the situation. He asks the scorpion: "Why did you do that? Not just me, but we both are going to die!" And the scorpion calmly replies: "Because I am a scorpion and that's what scorpions do. Scorpions sting frogs."

"Three things will last forever: faith, hope, and love - and the greatest of these is love." - Corinthians 13 -13

If you think it's impossible, it isn't

If you think you know everything, you don't...

If you think you're alone, you're not...

Jim Rohn –

**Chapter 4 – health**

"Health is not valued till sickness comes." Thomas Fuller

"To keep the body in good health is a duty, otherwise we shall not be able to keep our mind strong and clear." Buddha

When eating an elephant take one bite at a time - Creighton Abrams

The journey of a thousand miles begins with one step - Lao Tzu

Every failure is a lesson. If you are not willing to fail, you are not ready to succeed.

I do not understand what I do. For what I want to do I do not do, but what I hate I do. - Romans 7:15

Change happens in an instant, when our belief system changes.

## Chapter 5 - Relationships

"Forgiveness is giving up on the hope of ever having a better past."

"No man is an island entire of itself; every man

is a piece of the continent, a part of the main;

if a clod be washed away by the sea, Europe

is the less, as well as if a promontory were, as

well as any manner of thy friends or of thine

own were; any man's death diminishes me,

because I am involved in mankind.

And therefore, never send to know for whom

the bell tolls; it tolls for thee."

"We all deserve to be happy"

"Feel like a bad parent? The Australian Quokka, toss their babies at predators so they can escape.

## Autobiography in Five Chapters - by Portia Nelson

*Chapter One*

I walk down the street.

There is a deep hole in the sidewalk.

I fall in.

I am lost .... I am helpless.

It isn't my fault.

It takes forever to find a way out.

*Chapter Two*

I walk down the street.

There is a deep hole in the sidewalk.

I pretend that I don't see it.

I fall in again.

I can't believe I am in this same place.

But, it isn't my fault.

It still takes a long time to get out.

*Chapter Three*

I walk down the same street.

There is a deep hole in the sidewalk.

I see it is there.

I still fall in ... it's a habit ... but, my eyes are open.

I know where I am.

It is my fault.

I get out immediately.

*Chapter Four*

I walk down the same street.

There is a deep hole in the sidewalk.

I walk around it.

*Chapter Five*

I walk down another street.

The foundation of communication – Rapport

**Chapter 6 – Finances**

"Too many people spend money they haven't earned, to buy things they don't want, to impress people they don't like." Will Smith

"You can have everything in life you want, if you will just help other people get what they want." Zig Ziglar

The only stupid question is the one you don't ask!

"Live like no one else, so one day you can live like no one else." - David Ramsey

"The rich rule over the poor, and the borrower is slave to the lender." - Proverbs 22:7

"Money is not everything, but it ranks right up there with oxygen."

- Zig Ziglar

For the love of money is the root of all evil - Timothy 6:10

The Widow's Offering 41 Jesus sat down opposite the place where the offerings were put and watched the crowd putting their money into the temple treasury. Many rich people threw in large amounts. 42 But a poor widow came and put in two very small copper coins, worth only a few cents. 43 Calling his disciples to him, Jesus said, "Truly, I tell you, this poor widow has put more into the treasury than all the others. 44 They all gave out of their wealth; but she, out of her poverty, put in everything—all she had to live on." - Mark 12:41-44

## Chapter 7 – Personal Growth

"Where there is no vision, the people perish..." James 29:18

"A dead thing can go with the stream, but only a living thing can go against it." - G.K. Chesterton, The Everlasting Man

"For things to change, you have to change. To make yourself more attractive you have to become more attractive"

"Alice: Would you tell me, please, which way I ought to go from here?

The Cheshire Cat: That depends a good deal on where you want to get to.

Alice: I don't much care where.

The Cheshire Cat: Then it doesn't much matter which way you go."

-Lewis Carol, Alice In Wonderland

"Know Thyself" – The Oracle at Delphi

## Chapter 8 – Environment

"When a flower doesn't bloom, you fix the environment in which it grows, not the flower." - Alexander Den Heijer

"A place for everything and everything in **its** place."

"Action is the real measure of intelligence." - Napoleon Hill

## Chapter 9 – Career

"80% Of Life Is Just Showing Up" - Woody Allen

"Hard work beats talent every time."

"Do the work others aren't willing to do and you will get the things that others will never have."

"You can have everything in life you want, if you will just help other people get what they want." - Zig Ziglar

"The one thing you can't take away from me is the way I choose to respond to what you do to me. The last of one's freedoms is to choose one's attitude in any given circumstance." - Viktor E. Frankl (Author of Man's Search for Meaning and Holocaust survivor)

"Between stimulus and response there is a space. In that space is our power to choose our response. In our response lies our growth and our freedom" – Viktor E. Frankl

### Chapter 10 – Fun and Recreation

"All work and no play, makes Jack a dull boy" - James Howell

"Everyone deserves happiness"

Create in me a pure heart, O God, and renew a steadfast spirit within me. Do not cast me from your presence or take your Holy Spirit from me. Restore to me the joy of your salvation and grant me a willing spirit, to sustain me. - Psalm 51:10-12

"Where have all the good times gone?" - Van Halen

### Quotes from conclusion

"All good things must come to an end,"

We must love ourselves first so we can love others. When we love ourselves, we can reflect it outward to others.

We are not worth anything to anyone if we are not worth something to ourselves first.

Forgiveness is not for the other person forgiveness is for you.

We only control our choices.

We empower our lives not by what happens to us, but what we choose to do next in response.

Remember to breathe in deeply and let it out twice as slowly.

"Tis better to have loved and lost than never to have loved at all" - Alfred Lord Tennyson

"The significant problems we face cannot be solved at the same level of thinking (consciousness) we were at when we created them." - Albert Einstein

The only thing we have in this world is our word.

Notes:

_____

_____

_____

_____

_____

_____

_____

_____

# Appendix B
## Self-Development Tools

Wheel of Life Chart

3 P's

S.M.A.R.T. Goals

W.F.O. - Well Formed Outcome

Difficult Conversations

**Wheel of Life Chart**

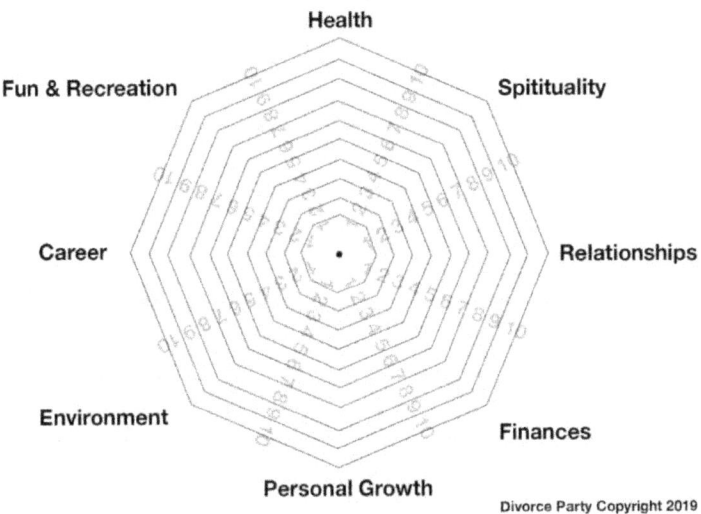

## The 3 P's

**P – Purpose** (a simple sentence or two about what this goal gets you)

_____

_____

**P – Products** (the outcomes and what evidence you want to produce / manifest both in the world, others and within yourself. What will you see, hear and feel?)

_____

_____

_____

_____

_____

**P – Process** – (the action steps written down in sequential order)

_____

_____

_____

_____

_____

## S.M.A.R.T. Goal (Meyer, 2019)

**What is the Goal?** (Written in the future tense as if already achieved)

_____

_____

_____

### S - Specific.

What will the goal accomplish?

_____

_____

_____

How and why will it be accomplished?

_____

_____

_____

### M - Measurable.

How will you measure whether or not the goal has been reached (list at least two indicators)?

_____

_____

_____

**A - Achievable.**

Is it possible?

_____
_____
_____

Have others done it successfully?

_____
_____
_____

Do you have the necessary knowledge, skills, abilities, and resources to accomplish the goal?

_____
_____
_____

Will meeting the goal challenge you without defeating you?

_____
_____
_____

**R - Results-focused.**

What is the reason, purpose, or benefit of accomplishing the goal?

_____
_____

What is the outcome result (not the activities leading up to the result) of the goal?

**T - Time-based.**

What is the established completion date and does that completion date create a practical sense of urgency?

Revised Goal:

**WFO – Well-Formed Outcome**

(O'Conner & Seymour, 2011)

The WFO is like the SMART goal but expanded. I look at the SMART goals as the quick and dirty but larger projects can benefit from the expanded depth of the WFO.

**WFO - Clarity**

What do you want?

_____

_____

_____

Can it be initiated by you?

_____

_____

Can it be controlled by you?

_____

_____

Is it large or manageable?

_____

_____

Chunk down if necessary.

_____

## WFO – Evidence

How will you know when you have it?

What will you see?

What will you hear?

How will you feel?

What might you smell or taste?

What will be different now that you have it?

**WFO – Context**

Where does it fit in your life?

When do you want it?

Where do you want it?

With whom do you want it?

_____

_____

Under what circumstances do you want it?

_____

_____

_____

## WFO – Other Considerations

What else in your life will be impacted?

_____

_____

_____

What positive and negative consequences may be created?

Positive –

_____

_____

_____

Negative –

_____

_____

_____

What resources do you have?
___
___
___

What resources do you need?
___
___
___

What are you already doing?
___
___
___

What will achieving this outcome do for you?
___
___
___
___
___
___

## WFO – Taking Action

How do you plan to be in action?

_____

_____

_____

Is there more than one way?

_____

_____

_____

What are they?

_____

_____

_____

What are your time frames?

_____

_____

_____

What stops you?

_____

_____

_____

How will you celebrate your success and learning?
_____
_____
_____

**WFO – Looking Ahead**

What do you see in the future?
_____
_____
_____

Step into the future having achieved the outcome.
_____
_____
_____

Describe how it feels.
_____
_____
_____

Reflect back on how you achieved the outcome.
_____
_____
_____

What supported you?

_____
_____
_____

Did anything get in the way?

_____
_____
_____

What might you do differently?

_____
_____
_____

**Difficult Conversations**

All feelings are valid. When working on conflict resolution sometimes it can be valuable to somewhat disassociate emotionally and look at conflict logically. Imagine there is a movie playing. The actors, you and someone else in the drama are on the movie screen. You are an observer in the front row of a theater watching the movie and the problem. You can see, hear and feel both points of view and you can see the big picture also, a view that each individual cannot see. You have a remote control that you can pause, rewind, fast forward and share with the other person in the conflict.

Roll the movie. Allow it flow timeless and simultaneous. You have a heightened sense of empathy, understanding and knowing. Everything you thought you knew and everything you know now. Jump into the movie as yourself. See what you saw, feel what you felt and hear what you heard. Play the movie of the problem start to finish. Start the movie at a safe place just a moment before the problem happened. Play from start to finish and let it roll just a few moments after the problem to a safe point to stop after the problem occurred. What do you notice? What is important to you about this problem? What is it that you want? What do you fear? What commitments were made, kept or broken by you or them? What is the other person in the conflict not seeing, hearing or feeling? What do you want to say to them?

_____

_____

_____

_____

_____

_____

_____

_____

_____

_____

_____

Jump out of the movie and back into your seat. Do you smell popcorn? I like Twizzlers myself. Okay, jump back into the movie as the other person. You are now that person. See what they see, feel what they feel and hear what they hear. Play the movie of the problem start to finish. Start the movie at a safe place just a moment before the problem happened. Play from start to finish and let it roll just a few moments after the problem to a safe point to stop after the problem occurred. What do you notice different from their perspective? What is important to you about this problem? What is it that you want? What do you fear? What commitments were made, kept or broken by you or them? What is the other person in the conflict not seeing, hearing or feeling? What do you want to say to them?

_____

_____

_____

_____

_____

_____

_____

_____

_____

_____

Jump out of the movie and back into your seat. Do you smell popcorn? I think someone burned the popcorn. Please stop talking during the movie. I don't want to miss the best part! Now let's watch the movie one more time. Play the movie of the problem start to finish. What do you notice that both people do not see? What is important about this problem? What is it that they want? What do they fear? What commitments were made, kept or broken by them? What is the other person in the conflict not seeing, hearing or feeling? What do you want to say to them?

_____

_____

_____

_____

_____

_____

_____

_____

_____

_____

_____

_____

_____

# DIVORCE PARTY

# APPENDIX C

**Exercises and Theory Explained**

3 P's Explained ............................................. 155

Conflict Resolution ........................................ 95

Difficult Conversations – Movie Screen Exercise ..... 92

Dreaded Drama Triangle – D.D.T. ...................... 75

Letting Go of Stress Exercise .......................... 200

Maslow's Hierarch of Needs ............................ 78

Mindful Breathing Exercise ............................. 36

Rapport .................................................. **xvii**

Relationship 3 Elements ................................ 83

S.M.A.R.T. Goal Theory ............................... 147

# Thank You!

David Youhas

2019

## - THE END -

# Acknowledgement

Thank you and appreciation to those who helped me in the process of writing the book or taught me or shaped my life in some way. He who has shaped my life and continues to do so the most of all, thanks be to God.

My children ... Andrew, Kimberlyn, Shelby and Haley ... You have all given me a powerful purpose and inspired me to strive to be a better father and person. I have learned more about living and the value of relationships because of you. You all inspire me to continue improving and reaching for beyond what is comfortable. I am so proud of each and every one of you. Your accomplishments, your uniqueness, your quirks, and all the things that make you, you. I am proud of how you all get back up and move forward, when life happens. I look forward to seeing all of your successes to come. I love you all.

Sister Alice - acknowledgement and in memory of this caring and tough woman. She took me fishing when my father and role models were not available, she brought me a vaporizer when I was sick, and we couldn't afford one. She was tough as nails and also cared and loved unconditionally.

Big Brother Organization and Big Brother Rick, for being an amazing role model and second family during a difficult time.

Neighbor John, you listened to me, and inspired me to be an entrepreneur.

Every failure, shortcoming, and mistake, thank you, thank you, thank you for helping me learn what not to do. There is no other way to become excellent. There is no failure, only feedback. ( :

Landmark Education - for getting me out of my drift, out of the bleachers, playing on the field and in the game.

QC1 – Barbara, David, Margee, and Joyce. - for one of the greatest training year of my life. Thank you for calling me on my stuff, holding me accountable and seeing something greater than I could see in myself. Thank you for the gift of learning about rapport.

RR NLP – Joyce, Nadine, and Kenna. "What other people think of you is none of your business."

The Divorce Care Program – helping me begin to heal.

David Ramsey - giving me hope when I didn't have any and transforming my life and my children's lives financially.

Thank you, Mary Frances Wright. My favorite/unfavorite class from high school was a beautiful and tragic "English" class taught by a wonderful woman Mary Frances Wright. This class was about the Holocaust and became and continues to be life changing. Other classes were interesting and some fun, but this class taught me the value of life. There has been no other class that I have carried with me every day since then. It continually shapes me and my lens of how I view the world, people, moments, how precious life is, and how moments and choices affect us. A book that has inspired me and is on my top 7 books list of "what books would you have with you if you were stranded on an island" - Man's Search for Meaning – by Viktor E. Frankl. The experiences in this book are a reflection of a horrible and tragic moment in time, a first-hand account by Viktor E. Frankl, neurologist, psychologist, Holocaust survivor and founder of the field of Logotherapy. I believe he was the right person, in the right place, at the right time, to see and observe something so unimaginably horrific, observe and learn and share his observations, how humans behave with and without a purpose and meaning of life. His observations, moving forward, have helped who knows how many people and helping those living with the challenges of life and how valuable having a purpose in life is. I so appreciate my teacher Mary Wright, who may not fully know how valuable that class was for me and others. Thank you, Mary, for all that you have done and continue to do as a powerful teacher, making a difference and how your teaching continues to send out ripples of fascination and a hunger to learn. And thank you, Mary, for seeing in me unlimited potential and possibility, and as someone and something more than I could see in myself. You also inspired me to believe that I have a voice and that I have something valuable to say. And here it is in this book. Thank you.

Thank you to my friends and supporters, from cheerleaders to critics and all of the diverse friends and communities that have allowed me in your inner circle. I travel fluently, quickly and expansively within relationships, communities, organizations, and I am always honored when allowed as a guest in a trusted circle. I value being a contributor and always want to add to others' lives and communities. Thank you for all of the often times that you have given and contributed to me. Thank you for challenging me, listening, a kind word, inspiring, critiquing, or just the quality time of your presence and connection. Thank you!

Lilia my Divorce Party book coach. Thank you for pushing me to get this done and all of your insightful advice from all of your experience as an author and a publisher.

My ex-wife Sara and her husband Paul. Thank you for being the best mother I could want for my children. You are an excellent mother. You have defended them like a mama bear and also you care for them and love them, for better or ... for the times they can be challenging. Thank you for your commitment to them and all that you do. Also, a shout out to stepdad Paul who has been helpful, empathetic, supportive and patient through the shared parenting ups and downs to raise and support the children/adults as they face the challenges of life. Thank you, Sara and Paul Hurlbut, (I got it right)!

# Bibliography

Allen, D. (2015). *Getting Things Done.* New York: Penguin Group.

*Cognitive dissonance.* (2019, December). Retrieved from Wikipedia: https://en.wikipedia.org/wiki/Cognitive_dissonance

Cousins, N. (1979). Anatomy of an Illness as Perceived by the Patient: Reflections on Healing and Regeneration. *The New England Journal of Medicine.*

Covey, S. (1995). *First Things First.* New York: Fireside.

Emerald, D. (2014). *The Power of T.E.D.* Bainbridge Island: Polaris Publishing.

*Financial Peace University.* (2019). Retrieved from David Ramsey: https://www.daveramsey.com/fpu

Frankl, V. E. (1959). *Man's Search for Meaning.* Cutchogue: Buccaneer Books Inc.

Hill, N. (1937). *Think and Grow Rich.* New York: Penguin Group.

Ramsey, D. (2019). *New Car vs Used Car.* Retrieved from Dave Ramsey: https://www.daveramsey.com/blog/new-car-vs-used-car

Robbins, A. (1994). *Giant Steps.* New York: Fireside.

Stephen B. Karpman, M. (1968). *FAIRY TALES AND SCRIPT DRAMA ANALYSIS.* Retrieved from Karpman Drama Triangle: https://en.wikipedia.org/wiki/Karpman_drama_triangle

Tracy, B. (2002). *Eat That Frog.* San Francisco: Berrett-Koehler Publishers, Inc.

Vivyan, C. (2009). *MindfuBreathing.* Retrieved from Get Self Help: https://www.getselfhelp.co.uk/docs/MindfulBreathing.pdf

# ABOUT THE AUTHOR
David Youhas

David' Amazon Author Page

Hello! I am David Youhas and the proud father of my 4 children. I have personally experienced the horrible experience of divorce and came out on the other side returning to a life of happiness, excitement and growth. My experience became the seeds for my own life change and this book.

One of my next biggest challenges, was my finances and I sought out help from a David Ramsey Financial Peace University program. There are so many available resources and programs for any challenges we face. But we must have the courage to ask for help and the persistence and determination to help ourselves, even when we don't feel like it.

I continued healing and found a love for helping others. I proactively pursued my own healing and training in performance and relationship coaching. And now I am a board registered master practitioner in coaching NLP, Hypnosis, and Time Line Therapy®. I am the host of the podcast, *Awaken The Mind* - The NLP and Hypnosis Guide.

About the Author – David Youhas Bio

Host of *Awaken the Mind* – The NLP and Hypnosis Guide www.nlpandhypnosisguide.com

Board Certified Master Practitioner in NLP through American Board of Neuro Linguistic Programming

Board Certified Master Practitioner Hypnotist through American Board of Hypnotherapy

Master Practitioner Time Line Therapy®

Board Certified Hypnotist through

National Guild of Hypnotists and the

International Association of Counselors and Therapists

You are not your past. Who are you really? You are unlimited future potential. What defines us is not what happened to us, but what we do next in response. What do we want instead? What matters is the action we take that moves us toward or away from that desired future AND persisting until we get it.

Going through the worst time of my life, I had a realization that I was responsible for my happiness. Through the challenges I faced, I focused on my health, lost over 100 pounds and ran 6 marathons in 2 years.

Owner of - Stop It Hypnosis - www.stopithypnosis.com

Owner - Ask- Coach - www.ask-coach.com

<u>Media background</u>

- Owner of - David Youhas Photography

www.davidyouhasphotography.com

- Graduate of the New York Institute of Photography

- N.Y.I.P. – Professional Photography

- Professional photographer for the Illinois Marathon in Champaign at the University of Illinois

- Published work in Concrete Decor Magazine.

Certified - Performance Coach

Certified - Relationship Coach

Certified - Master Vision Board Coach

<u>Additional Training Includes</u>

Landmark Education – Forum and Advanced

Steven Covey – Franklin Covey

Napoleon Hill – Leadership training

Resource Realization – performance coaching, NLP, Discover, Focus

Source Point – Relationship coaching certification

Tadd James, NLP, Hypnosis and Time Line Therapy®

David Elman Hypnosis Institute Certification

Jason Linett – Sheila Granger Virtual Gastric Band Certification
Freddy Jacquin - Arrow Technique

Bob Burns - Swan Technique Certification

Melissa Tiers - Anxiety Tools, Life Coaching and Integrative Hypnosis Certification

Please let me know your thoughts about this book. My intention is to continually sharpen the saw of excellence and to create a powerful and valuable resource for those experiencing divorce, separation and break ups. To get you to move from where you are now to where you want to be instead. Sign up for our email list and get involved in our social groups here: www.divorcepartykeys.com

www.ingramcontent.com/pod-product-compliance
Lightning Source LLC
Chambersburg PA
CBHW060940230426
43665CB00015B/2006